To Paul,

The finest Judge
in the Commonwealth of Kentucky

Tony

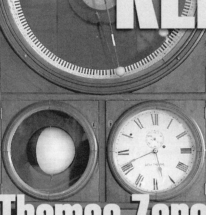

TIME KEEPER

Thomas Zane Roberts
A Kentucky Renaissance Man

Anthony W. Frohlich

Cover design and book layout by Asher Graphics
Celestial Clock photos by Deogracias Lerma

Manufactured in the United States of America

All book order correspondence should be addressed to:

Enchanted Valley Publishing Company
9253 Old Union Rd.
Union, KY 41091

859-384-4929

Dedicated to the memory of
Ralph Zane Cason

FOREWORD

Thomas Zane Roberts was born on a farm in Middle Creek, Boone County, Kentucky on October 4, 1851. He lived on Middle Creek his entire life. He died on January 15, 1925 at the age of 73 years. He was an inventor, teacher, farmer, miller, musician, carpenter, horologist, astronomer, poet, author and painter. He is best known for his "solar clock," which he built out of hand tools in a shed beside his house and unveiled in 1913. It continues to work properly to this day without repair. People have come from all over the United States and the world to see this marvelous work.

Roberts' home still exists on Middle Creek. The Middle Creek valley is six miles from the county seat of Burlington and is situated between Burlington and Belleview. It was one of the earliest settlements in Boone County. It is in the proximity of Petersburg and Belleview, which were early Ohio River ports.

The Middle Creek area has been called The Enchanted Valley. Much of the area retains its same rustic appearance of 200 years ago. A large part of this area has been preserved. It is the home of the Dinsmore homestead, one of the finest plantations in early Boone County. The plantation house still stands intact as a museum along with many other structures. The Boone Fiscal Court created the Middle Creek Park. The Middle Creek Park of 181 acres lies in the Middle Creek valley. The Boone Conservancy owns 129 acres, which they purchased from the Camargo Hunt Club, a fox hunting club. In 2005 it purchased an additional adjacent 44 acres for a park containing a large lake. The Nature Conservancy, a nonprofit organization devoted to the preservation of ecologically and environmentally important areas, owns the Boone County Cliff Nature Preserve, which once was part of the farm of Thomas Zane Roberts and upon which Roberts' observatory stood so he could study the planets. The cliffs are huge conglomerate deposits left by glaciers some 700,000 years ago and represent the finest glacier deposit in Kentucky.

There are many people to thank for their assistance. When I began this project in the 1970s, Candy, my wife, helped me in the original research. We spent many winter days together looking through old newspapers and other documents in the unheated attic of the old building housing the Burlington Hardware Store and the *Boone County Recorder*, located at the corner of Burlington Pike and Idlewild Road. Ralph Cason spent many hours sharing stories with me about his Uncle Tom Roberts and Middle Creek as well as allowing me the full run of Uncle Tom's house, his documents, the buildings and farm. Dorotha Griesser, the grandniece of Uncle Tom, also shared her experiences of her great uncle, Tom Roberts, as well as providing unfettered access to the documents in her possession. Marty McDonald, the executive director of Dinsmore, and Cathy Collopy, its research director, provided assistance and insight on the chapter about the Dinsmore plantation. Thanks to Karen Claiborne, Diane Nichols, also known as "The Zane Lady," and Amy Kastigar of the Ohio County Public Library in Wheeling, West Virginia, for their help in the genealogy of the family. A special thank you to Bridget Striker, research director for the Boone County Library, who always had time for me. Many thanks to my assistants, Brooke Buchanan, Carol Long and David Spaulding. To all those who provided assistance, I am truly grateful.

Anthony W. Frohlich

UNCLE TOM'S CLOCK

May 27, 1949   Clock built in 1913

Uncle Tom built a clock, eight feet three inches tall,
And started it running by the dining room wall.
For thirty-six years its ticked seconds away;
Showing month, day, and hour, minutes, seconds each day.

And it shows you the moon, sun, and stars in the sky;
It's so perfect that not even leap year gets by.
The cabinet he made out of walnut rails;
It took axe, saw, and plane, screws, hammer, and nails.

For two years he labored, but just in spared time,
Not a soul knew the meaning of his project sublime;
He figured on paper, boards, and finally a slate.
To get all the ratios accurate, and right on the date.

In the round box called the sun, are eighteen cogs cut out of brass,
Which he figured and cut so that planets could pass
In the order they travel in their path in the sky,
And their difference in speed is timed perfect. Oh My!

The moon changes constantly, as it does in the sky—
Showing all of its phases to those who pass by;
Then the days of the week are shown perfectly clear,
Not one thing was forgotten; and we treasure each year.

All is run from the clock; with shafts leading each way,
Two weights are the means of its power and sway.
The knowledge and patience to figure it all
Is too great to be measured, till at the last call.

People have come from all over the land;
To look at this wonder, and hear of the man—
Who wanted so much to do what was right,
That he studied and watched, both by day and by night.

That he might build a clock, that would keep him in pace;
So when Sunday came round, he would be in his place
As a teacher of Sunday School and director of song,
Yes, he served Jesus faithfully all his life long.

By
   Dorotha Griesser
   (grandniece to T.Z. Roberts)

TABLE OF CONTENTS

CHAPTER ONE

THE SOLAR CLOCK

Thomas Zane Roberts is best known for his masterpiece, the solar clock. The association has shadowed many of the other accomplishments of his life. In fact, a local folklore has developed over the years embracing Roberts and the origin of the clock. The story goes something like this:

> Roberts was working in the field one Sunday not realizing that it was the Sabbath. Fellow church members, certain Roberts was sick because he wasn't at Church, stopped at the Middle Creek farm to satisfy their premonitions. Upon arriving they were surprised to find Roberts working away with healthful vigor. When they inquired of Roberts why he was working on Sunday and was not present at Church, he supposedly replied that he had apparently lost track of the days, because he wasn't aware that it was the Sabbath. The myth continues that Roberts, being the conscientious churchgoer that he was, resolved to do something about the situation right then and there. He went out and purchased a telescope and built a lookout tower on the hill behind his house. The instant astronomer studied the planets for a year, and used his findings to make the calculations needed in constructing the clock. He then secretly spent another year building a foolproof timepiece, which was quietly unveiled in the kitchen of his home in 1913.[1]

The legend draws upon actual experiences in Roberts' life but distorts them in such a way as to deprive the listener the opportunity to fully appreciate the creative abilities of this man. His astronomical knowledge and abilities as a horologist were self-taught. His mathematical abilities and craftsmanship are clearly evident in this masterpiece. The clock was a creation born out of skills developed over a lifetime. One can best start with reviewing Roberts' development in the field of horology.

The construction of the solar clock was not Roberts' first experience working with clocks. His diary shows that he was interested in clocks at least as early as 1882. During that period of time Roberts was teaching at the Frogtown School. In those days Frogtown was too far to travel from Middle Creek each day, so during the school term he boarded with the Dobbins family. He made a notation on January 28, 1882 that he cleaned Mr. Dobbins' clock. Although cleaning a clock is certainly not the same as building one, this shows Roberts' interest in clocks began much earlier than the construction of the solar clock.

On December 7 of the next year Roberts spent a rainy day fixing a clock in his home. The indication seems to be that he was working on his own clock. What makes this more interesting is a passage he recorded six months earlier on March 25: "I forgot today was Sunday – so I worked till noon before I found it out." A review of Roberts' diary, maintained from October 4, 1872 through March of 1909, shows this date was the only time he missed church on the Sabbath.

Roberts did in fact build a smaller clock before he built the solar clock. Josephine Cason was the wife of Ralph Cason, Roberts' nephew. Shortly after Ralph and Josephine Cason were married on December 24, 1912 , they moved in with Roberts at the Middle Creek home and lived with Roberts until his death. The Casons lived in the same home until their deaths.[2] They were the first persons to see the solar clock as it was against the kitchen wall when they moved in with Roberts.

Josephine Cason wrote a paper about Roberts and maintains that he did in fact build a smaller clock before building the solar clock:

> He began by building a calendar clock that would tell him the day of the week, as he said sometimes he would get mixed up when living alone and forget when Sunday came. Some tell on him that one Sunday morn he was working away on the place when one of his neighbors came along and asked him why he was working on Sunday. Why he said, "Is it Sunday?" And when the neighbor convinced him it was Sunday he laid (his grubbing hoe) I think it was, and went to the house. So this set him to studying on a clock that would tell the day of the week, and he soon studied out and built a small clock...."[3]

Roberts still had the calendar clock on February 21, 1893 because he recorded in his diary that he fixed it. Sometime after that date Roberts gave the clock to George Koons, who moved to an adjoining farm in 1913, the same year the solar clock was unveiled. It is easy to understand how the solar clock mythology would adopt the "missing of Church" story since the calendar clock was no longer in the Roberts' household.

In 1975 Ralph Cason took this author to see the calendar clock. Ralph Cason had been the administrator of the estate of George Koons. At that time, as now, the clock is owned by Isabelle Rowland. Upon George Koons' death the clock passed to his daughter, Ida Koons. Upon Ida's death in 1974, her great-niece Isabelle Rowland received the clock as a beneficiary of her estate. Ralph Cason was also the executor of Ida Koons' estate.

The clock was typical of its day. The inner workings were not made by Roberts but by the Seth Thomas Clock Company of Connecticut. In order to maximize production and maintain lower shipping costs, Connecticut clockmakers sent only the essential inner workings (aka the movement) of the clocks to the consumer. The purchaser of the clocks relied upon local cabinetmakers to construct the remainder of the clock.[4] Roberts was an excellent carpenter, and one can easily understand his choice of this time-piece.

The clock is of the shelf variety. It is 27 inches tall, 13 1/2 inches wide, and 4 inches in width. It was powered by an eight-day pendulum motor with brass works. The clock consisted of two dials perpendicular with the base. The uppermost dial showed the time marked off in hours, represented by Roman numerals. The lower face was a dial that showed the day of the month. The calendar dial was marked off from 1 to 31 to show the day of the month, and it also indicated the day of the week. In months where there were fewer than 31 days, it was necessary to set the dial hand forward to correct the clock for the ensuing month. The Seth Thomas Clock Company patented this calendar attachment in 1876, so it was still relatively new when Roberts built the clock in 1883. The clock also had a striking mechanism, which resounded on the hour the number of times directly proportionate to that hour.

Roberts wrote in his diary on January 15, 1885 that he "mend Jim Merchant's clock." Roberts had been appointed guardian of Jim Merchant by order of the Boone County Court on June 14, 1877. There is no indication that Roberts worked on clocks any further until his undertaking to build the solar clock. Horology was never a commercial enterprise but simply a practical hobby through which he gained knowledge about clocks and their inner workings.

The mythology of the solar clock held that Roberts bought a telescope, studied the planets for a year, and built his creation with that sole knowledge gained from the hill behind his house. Like the "missing Church on Sunday" anecdote, this also is misleading. Roberts bought his telescope in Cincinnati on March 18, 1902, at least seven years before he began working on the solar clock. The power of the telescope is not known. In his will he bequeathed the telescope to his nephew Hugh French in 1925, and its whereabouts at this time is a mystery. The seven years that Roberts studied the planets offers a more realistic experience than the one year the mythology offers.

Although Roberts was an amateur astronomer, his seriousness for this field of science cannot be doubted. He began his pursuit of astronomy by observing the stars from the roof of his house but determined this was inadequate to his purposes. He constructed an observatory high on the hill behind his house which is now part of the Boone County Cliffs Nature Preserve. The observatory was 30 feet high.[5] Roberts built the observatory large enough to seat 12 people. Roberts said it proved an immeasurable improvement over his earlier practice. When perched aloft in his observatory, Roberts claimed he could watch his sister feed the chickens on her farm in Aurora, Indiana.[6]

Ruth Kelly was a neighbor of Roberts. Her father, Charles Kelly and Roberts were good friends, and their fathers were friends. Two of Roberts' siblings married relatives of the Kelly family. Kelly remembered the telescope well, described it as "good sized" and said "I imagine he had the most powerful telescope of his day." She recalled that Roberts would bring the telescope to their farm, which was one of the highest points in Boone County. He would place the telescope on a tripod, and he and her father would look at various things through it. She recalled one time Roberts saying to her father, "Now Charley, that little speck we see is the cupola on the Burlington Courthouse."[7]

Personal experience with his telescope was not the only source of Roberts' astronomical knowledge. Roberts' father had been a justice of the peace and maintained a book of his court cases. Paper being rare in those days, Roberts "reused" this book with his own writing and thoughts, and pasted items of interest in this book. It contained articles concerning the royal astronomer of England as well as articles regarding the Royal Astronomical Society. Whether articles such as these or others' research served as a basis for his calculations for the planetarium in the solar clock, or if his calculations were derived solely from his observations is difficult to discern. The assumption is that a combination of his personal observations and secondary research contributed to the development of the solar clock. However, credit for applying the calculations to the workings of the solar clock belongs entirely to Roberts. Some of these calculations appear in his father's justice of the peace record book. After consuming his available supply of paper, Roberts turned to using boards to write on. He felt this burdensome, so he purchased a slate upon which he developed his final formulas.[8] Despite these impediments, Roberts' work was extremely accurate. To testify to its accuracy is the proof of time, as the solar clock has never failed to function correctly.

Ruth Kelly remembers Roberts and her father were "always talking about some mathematical problem or something or another." She recalled that Roberts was working on the formulas for the clock for years before he started construction. She recalled the first small clock he built and that Roberts spoke for years of building the solar clock. . Kelly said:

> . . . I always thought and I'm sure my father thought that he just did it because he wanted to. He had the potential to do it and he wanted to see it. And I believe he—I know he had this in the back of his mind for years because it was—my father said he talked to him about it for years before he put anything on paper, you know, about the mathematical calculations . . .[9]

Why or exactly when the 60-year-old Roberts decided to build this clock remains a mystery. Josephine Cason wrote that the reason was because Roberts simply wanted an improved clock over his earlier calendar clock. Neither Roberts' diary nor any of his own writings suggest any other reasons for building the solar clock. No one knew he was building the clock until Ralph and Josephine Cason moved in and saw it in the kitchen of the Roberts home in February of 1913.

The solar clock folklore relates it took about two years to build the clock- one year for planet watching and calculation, and one year of construction. However, a newspaper article written three years after Roberts' death reports it took five years to construct the clock.[10] For 36 years, from October 4, 1872 until May of 1908, Roberts steadfastly kept his diary. After May of 1908 the next entry is March 1909, when he simply wrote, "Commenced keeping house alone in the shop." The shop refers to his workshop, which was adjacent to his house and contained his tools. We know he had "ceiled" the shop in January of 1904, assuming to make it livable. If this last entry of March 1909 indicates Roberts was commencing construction of the clock, then this 10-month interval probably holds the mystery of why he decided to build it. Josephine Cason wrote Roberts spent a year just working out the mathematical ratios to make the clock work and then built the machinery capable of building the cogs before he started working on the clock itself.[11]

During this period of time there was much speculation as to what Roberts was doing. The rumor was he was building an airplane. The neighbors had seen him using the telescope extensively, and news of the Wright brothers' success at Kitty Hawk, North Carolina in 1903, and their subsequent experiments at Dayton, Ohio had reached the inhabitants of Boone County.[12]

Perhaps just as many people were surprised to discover the solar clock when it was unveiled. Measuring 7 foot, 8 1/4 inches high and 34 inches wide, it contained basically four sections: the planetarium, the lunarium, the Seth Thomas timepiece, and a dial showing the days of the week. The most integral and vital section of the clock was the Seth Thomas clock works. It provided the motive power for all the other sections of the clock. The works of the timepiece consisted of an eight-day spring motor, a large pendulum, and a second weight-fall that required it be raised twice yearly, which was responsible for providing the extra power needed to drive the planetarium. Roman numerals on the clock face represented the hours, and a smaller dial located within the clock face ticked off the seconds.

The most fascinating section of the clock was the planetarium. By far the largest section of the clock, it had a diameter of 2 feet, 8 inches, and was 8 1/4 inches deep. The depth of the remainder of the clock is 7 3/4 inches. The planetarium is an abbreviated model of the earth's solar system. Located in the center of the planetarium is a gold-colored disc, which represents the sun. Rotating around the sun are four spheres the size of golf balls. The spheres represent the planets Earth, Mars, Venus and Jupiter. Each sphere is located in the planetarium at a scaled distance from the Sun and the other planets mirroring the solar system. The circumference of the planetarium is marked off in months and days, and thus it is possible to tell the day of the year by looking at the position of the planet Earth. On any given day one could find where these four planets were in relation to each other as well as to the sun.

Roberts' choice of the second, third, fourth and fifth planet in the solar system was remarkable. This was twenty years before the discovery of Pluto. Roberts rejected the use of the closest planet to the sun, Mercury, and scientists have little concern for it because of its deadly temperatures, which range from 670 degrees Fahrenheit on the side that faces the sun to 460 degrees below zero on the dark side. The planets that Roberts did incorporate in his miniature solar system are the ones that generate the greatest interest from space scientists.

The planetarium, like the rest of the clock, has never failed to work properly. There has not been a need to open the clock and thus its contents have never been exposed. How the planetarium works only Roberts knew. For power of movement the planetarium relies on the Seth Thomas works, with additional energy provided by the weight-fall that requires winding twice yearly. There were 18 cogs fashioned by hand and hidden within the gold disc, whose interaction propelled the planets. In the back of his diary Roberts explained the dimensions of the cog wheels and overall "error factor." Venus hand gains one degree of arc in 1,656 days, Mars hand loses one degree of arc in 46 years, Jupiter hand gains one degree in 250 years, and Earth hand gains one day in four years (which compensates for leap year). The dimensions of each individual cog and the dimensions of the steps of the cogs were so small (for example, the size of the step in the Mars driver cog is 102/1000 of an inch) that it is difficult to conceive how Roberts accomplished this feat.

In June of 1969 Roberts' workshop was inspected by J.M. Huchabee, a professional horologist for the magazine *American Horologist and Jeweler*. The workshop still contained discarded pieces from the construction of the solar clock. His summarization was the following:

> . . .we looked over the remnants of the shop. There yet remains a small box of odd brass wheels mostly unfinished. Some cams and star wheels are indexed in sevens, probably parts for the calendar. Pinions were of the lantern type and a few spoiled pieces indicate the wheels were hand cut with a file. An overhead shaft indicates some form of power tools were used, but there is no evidence of their type.[13]

The shaft Mr. Huchabee referred to was part of a crude metal lathe used in the cutting of the cogs for the planetarium. In 1969 only the shaft, which measured about 5 feet in diameter, remained of the lathe.

A third display of the clock was the lunarium. It is below the planetarium and to the left of the Seth Thomas timepiece. This feature was a replica of the Earth's moon, being a bit larger than a grapefruit. Its function was to report the inconstant phases of the moon by revealing the appropriate portions of its white and black hemispheres. It rotated on an axis recessed in the cabinet, which is invisible to the observer of the clock. Roberts also disclosed the measurements of the lunarium in the back of his diary. From these specifications it is known that the lunarium is intrinsically dependent on both the planetarium and Seth Thomas timepiece to operate correctly.

The lowest dial on the solar clock is the section that illustrates the days of the week. The dial is divided into 14 segments, representing the seven days of the week and their diurnal and nocturnal hours. The diurnal hours are represented by the written symbols on white. The nocturnal hours are represented by gold segments. The dial is read counterclockwise. Like all other readouts, this section never varied in its accuracy.

To ensure that the clock would never stop, Roberts installed an alarm system in the clock. Before the weight-fall can come to rest on the bottom of the clock cabinet and thus stop, it touches a wooden pedal. Pressure on this pedal causes a bell to begin ringing, and the ringing does not stop until the pressure of the weight-fall is removed, which is accomplished by rewinding the weight-fall. Sometimes the family had to get up in the middle of the night to rewind the clock because the alarm was so loud it was impossible to sleep.[14] Roberts also installed a lighting system in the clock so the planetarium could be illuminated. This was done even before the Roberts home had electricity.

As well as being a meticulous mechanic, Roberts also was a master carpenter. The casement to the clock is made of walnut. Roberts carefully chose the walnut boards from his Middle Creek farm. The wood was chosen for its intrinsic value as well as for its extrinsic beauty. Each piece of wood had its own particular history. Some came from furniture in his home or from particular places on the farm. Roberts could recite a story about each piece of wood in the clock casement. The stories have faded in memories, although the two panels in the door that covered the pendulum and alarm were made from walnut fence rails on the farm Roberts said were 75 years old.[15]

Josephine Cason wrote that Roberts was not satisfied with the clock, and at his death he was working on a clock "he said was more perfect than the first one."[16] This clock was to have a striking mechanism. However, his death in 1925 prevented Roberts from constructing this clock.

The first clock built by Thomas Zane Roberts in 1883.

The Planetarium.

*The Lunarium, the Seth Thomas timepiece,
and the weekdays dial.*

Inside lower door shows pendulum, alarm and weight-fall.
Notice wooden pedal to alarm system at lower left.

Shaft to metal lathe that hung in Roberts' workshop.

176   *Planetarium.*

Venus. dr cogs 39 Diam 1.$\frac{24}{100}$ in Step of Cogs $\frac{1}{10}$ in

     follower Cogs 60. Diam 1.$\frac{91}{100}$ Step $\frac{1}{10}$ in

venus hand gains 1 degree of arc in 1656 days

Earth dr. Cogs 28 Diam $\frac{9}{10}$ in step of cog $\frac{101}{1000}$ in

     follower Cogs 70 Diam 2$\frac{1}{5}$ in Step $\frac{101}{1000}$ in

earth hand gains 1 day in 4 yrs.

Mars dr. Cogs 17 Diam $\frac{55}{100}$ in Step of Cogs $\frac{102}{1000}$ in.

     follower Cogs 80 Diam . 2$\frac{6}{10}$ in step of Cogs $\frac{102}{1000}$ in

mars hand loses 1 degree of arc in 46 years.

Jupiter driver cogs 15 Diam $\frac{4722}{10000}$ in step of Cogs $\frac{1}{10}$ in

     Reducing wheel, cogs 75 Diam 2.$\frac{387}{1000}$ in Step $\frac{1}{10}$ in

     Second dr cogs 15 D &c same as above. Idle wheel about 30 cogs

     follower Cogs 89 Diam 2.$\frac{83}{100}$ in step $\frac{1}{10}$ in

Jupiter hand gains 1 degree in 250 years.

            Lunarium.

on minute hand staff dr 8 cogs into 72 cog on which shaft

are two drivers, 8 cog into 72 cog on which is 20 gog bevel meshing

into same size on lateral shaft on which is 8 cog bevel meshing

into 70 cog on globe shaft. The other driver is 12 cog

into 64 cog on which is 20 cog bevel meshing into bevel of same

size on vertical shaft running the Planetarium.

Roberts' handwritten notes on the cogs in the planetarium and lunarium.

CHAPTER TWO

ARRIVAL IN BOONE COUNTY

It was the 1830s when the Thomas Roberts family came to Burlington, the county seat of Boone County, Kentucky. Kentucky had been established as a state on June 1, 1792. Boone County was carved out of Campbell County in 1798 and was officially established on June 17, 1799. The first county seat was established at what was known as Craig's Camp, and upon becoming the county seat the name was changed to Wilmington. In 1816 the name was changed to Burlington.[1]

Some of the founding fathers of Boone County were inhabitants of Middle Creek and were still present when the Roberts family came to Burlington. The first entry in the first Order Book of Boone County states:

> At a meeting of sundry inhabitants of the county of Boone at the house of William Cave, Esquire, in the said County, on Monday, the 27th day of June, 1799 a commission of peace was produced from under the hand of James Garard, Esquire Governor of Kentucky, appointing John Hall, John Conner, John Brown, Archibald Huston and Archibald Reid, Esquires, Gentlemen Justices of the Peace of the County Court in the County of Boone. Whereupon the said John Conner administered the oath of office as a Justice of the Peace to the said John Hall and the said John Hall administered the same to the said John Conner, John Brown, Archibald Huston and Archibald Reid, Esquires, thereupon a Court was established.[2]

Cave Johnson was elected clerk of the court. Thomas Allen had been appointed coroner by the governor. John Cave qualified and took the oath of office as sheriff. Moses Scott qualified as surveyor. As well as being the first county surveyor, Moses Scott was also the first clerk of the Middle Creek Baptist Church.[3] He also served as Boone County's representative in the Kentucky legislature. The new county court had many duties including the creation of new roads, approval of grist mills, and establishment of government. One of the first actions was to lay the county into two districts, and the beginning point was designated as the mouth of Middle Creek. Robert Garnett had been operating a mill on Middle Creek for some time, and his water grist mill was the first one officially approved by the county court to dam a water way. In their book, *Boone County, Kentucky County Court Orders 1799-1815*, Stephen W. Worrel and Anne W. Fitzgerald determined the county court dealt with 975 matters during that period, of which 408 actions dealt with roads. A review of those road records reveals most of them, in some way or another, intersected the Middle Creek roads. When the first circuit court grand jury ever empaneled in Boone County returned its first indictment, it concerned Middle Creek:

> Dicky Berkshire, surveyor of the road from Livingston's Landing on the Ohio passing Garnett's Mill to where the road leaves Middle Creek, "for failing to keep the same in good repair." [4]

When Thomas and Roxanna Roberts, parents of Thomas Zane Roberts, came to Boone County in the 1830s, they were part of the westward migration occurring during the early years of the United States. Thomas was born in New Jersey. His mother was Martha Zane, and his father was John L. Roberts.[5] Their ancestors had arrived in New Jersey in the 1600s. [6]

Many of the descendants of Thomas Roberts have used Zane as part of their name. It has been considered a tribute to their ancestry. One newspaper article published in 1928, shortly after the death of Thomas Zane Roberts, reported Martha Zane was the daughter of the Zane who founded Zanesville, Ohio.[7] Another newspaper article claimed they were the descendants of Betty Zane.[8]

Author Zane Grey was the great-grandson of Ebenezer Zane, who founded Zanesville, Ohio. Zane Grey authored 89 books and is considered the father of the western novel. One hundred and four motion pictures were produced based upon his books.[9] His first three books were based upon his ancestors' exploits in the Ohio River country. The books were *Betty Zane, The Spirit of the Border,* and *The Lost Trail.* Zane Grey wrote that he was in possession of the private journals of Ebenezer Zane.[10] A short review of the Zane family exploits will show why the family is proud to carry on the family name.

Robert Zane arrived in New Jersey from England in 1678. He was a member of the Society of Friends or "Quakers." He settled in a place he called Newton. This New Jersey town is a short distance from Philadelphia. He had several children.[11] His grandson, William Andrew Zane (son of Nathaniel Zane) was expelled from the Society of Friends for marrying outside the Quaker faith. He and his wife migrated to the Potomac valley in present-day West Virginia. He had six children- Silas, Ebenezer, Jonathan, Andrew, Isaac and Betty. Ebenezer and his brothers, Jonathan and Silas, explored the Ohio wilderness and in 1769 built cabins at Wheeling Creek, West Virginia. They became famous Indian fighters. Their fortified home at the mouth of the creek became a favorite stopping place in the wilderness. The Zane stockade eventually developed into Fort Henry.[12]

Ebenezer Zane fought in the Indian wars and became a colonel in the Revolutionary War. In 1796 Congress authorized Ebenezer Zane to open a road through the forests of the Ohio country. It would become known as Zane's Trace and would become a much-traveled roadway. It became part of the National Road in 1825. Ebenezer's brothers, Jonathan and Silas, assisted him. Congress granted Ebenezer three lots, each a mile square, for his efforts. Two of the lots are now known as Zanesville (named after Ebenezer) and Lancaster, Ohio. The third was across the river from Chillicothe, Ohio. Zanesville served as the capital of Ohio from 1810-1812. Chillicothe served as the capital from 1803-1810 and from 1812-1816. [13]

Betty Zane became famous in history at the second siege of Wheeling (later Fort Henry) in 1782. On September 11, 1782, 300 Indians and 50 to 100 British soldiers known as the Queen's Rangers marched to the fort and demanded surrender. They were under the command of Simon Girty.

Silas Zane was selected with a Mr. Sullivan to manage the defense of the fort. Betty Zane, who had been sent to Philadelphia for her education, had recently come to Fort Henry. The most commonly accepted version of her exploit is set forth as follows:

> Fort Henry stood upon the bank of the Ohio, about a quarter of a mile above the mouth of Wheeling creek. Between it and the steep hill, on the east, were thirty log huts, which the Indians occupied and challenged the garrison to surrender. Colonel Shepherd refused and the attack commenced. From sunrise until noon the fire on both sides was constant, when that of the assailants slackened. Within the fort the only alarm was want of powder, and then it was remembered that a keg was concealed in the house of Ebenezer Zane, some sixty yards distant. It was determined to make an effort to obtain it, and the question "Who will go?" was proposed. At this crisis a young woman, sister of Ebenezer & Silas Zane, came forward and desired to be permitted to go. This proposition seemed so extravagant that it was refused, but she renewed it with earnestness, replying that the danger was the identical reason that induced her to offer, for the garrison was very weak and no solder's life should be placed in jeopardy, and if she were to fall her loss would not be felt. Her petition was finally granted and the gate

opened for her to pass out. This attracted the attention of several Indians who were straggling through the village. Their eyes were upon her as she crossed the open space to reach her brother's house, but whether they were seized with a feeling of clemency, or believing that a woman's life was not worth a load of gunpowder cannot be explained, suffice it, they permitted her to pass without molestation. When she reappeared, however, with the powder in her arms, suspecting the character of the burden, they fired at her as she swiftly glided toward the gate, but their balls flew wide of their mark and the brave Elizabeth Zane reached the fort in safety with her prize, and won a glorious name in history.[14]

While Ebenezer, Jonathan and Silas earned reputations as great Indian fighters who helped to open the Ohio country to settlers, perhaps brother Isaac's story is the most interesting. The Wyandot Indians captured him at 9 years of age. At age 18 he married Chief Tarhe's daughter Myeerah. Isaac was called "The White Eagle of the Wyandots." He was instrumental in bringing peace between the U.S. government and the Indians. Congress granted Isaac two large sections of land for his services. He settled in the Mad River Valley and built a great fort. It was called Zanestown and is now known as Zanesfield, Ohio.[15]

The exact relationship between Thomas Zane Roberts and the famous Zane family has never been precisely determined. In 1951 Myra N. Martin, a descendant of Jonathan Zane, began a work that she published in 1964.[16] She had possession of many original documents, including family Bibles. She undertook her task because she found so many errors in the published research of others. She concluded her work with the statement, "The tangled threads in the Zane history may never be unraveled." What makes the early Zane research difficult is that the New Jersey census records prior to 1830 were destroyed. There is much research published on the Zane/Roberts family that is simply incorrect. While this author has his opinions after many years of research on the Thomas Zane ancestry, only that which is beyond dispute is provided in this book.

Martha Zane was born in April 1785 in New Jersey.[17] She married John L. Roberts. John and Martha had three children born in New Jersey: Thomas (d.o.b. September 17, 1806); Benjamin (d.o.b. March 1, 1808); and Simeon (d.o.b. February 1810). Two children were born in Ohio, James Madison (d.o.b. December 2, 1821) and Martha Ann (September 1, 1822). Ohio census records show other male children lived with them.

As can be seen by the birthplaces of the children, John and Martha left New Jersey after Simeon's birth in 1810. They settled at Rossville in Butler County, Ohio by 1820. Their most probable path was by boat from Wheeling, West Virginia by way of the Ohio River and continuing on the Great Miami River.

One of the famous persons in the early history of the westward migration from the 13 colonies was John Symmes. He was a resident of Newton, Sussex County, New Jersey. Symmes fought in the American Revolution and was a delegate to the Continental Congress. In 1794, he and several others purchased 248,000 acres in Ohio, which included the present-day cities of Cincinnati and Dayton, Ohio as well as Butler County, Ohio. Symmes was one of the judges for the Northwest Territory. He served as lieutenant governor of New Jersey. His daughter, Anna, married General William Henry Harrison, later to become the President of the United States of America. [18] Symmes was the first owner of land north of the Ohio River between the Great Miami River and the Little Miami River. [19] He built his 16-room mansion at North Bend, overlooking the Ohio River not far from the mouth of the Great Miami River and across the Ohio River from Boone County, Ky. President Harrison and his wife would later acquire this estate.

William Henry Harrison was elected in Cincinnati, Ohio in 1799 as the territorial delegate to the U.S. Congress. He became chairman of the committee on public lands in the U.S. House of Representatives. He is credited with opening up the Northwest Territory to the common people by getting passed the Harrison

Land Act of 1800. People could buy land from the government with $160 dollars down and the balance paid over four years. Harrison would later serve as the representative of Butler, Warren, and Hamilton County, Ohio in the U.S. House of Representatives. Two of his children would marry residents of the city of Hamilton.[20] His granddaughter would marry John and Martha's son James Madison Roberts.

Rossville started in April 1801 when the government placed the land west of the Great Miami River on sale in Cincinnati. One of the early purchasers of a large section of that land was Thomas Roberts of the Northwest Territory. [21] In 1810 only 84 people lived in Rossville. [22]

John Roberts and family appear in the 1820 census in Butler County, Ohio. However, John Roberts does not appear in the 1830 census, and there is no record found that shows he purchased real estate in Rossville. His last child was born in 1822. He apparently died in the early 1820s. Martha and the children lived with Benjamin according to the 1830 census. By the 1840 census, Benjamin was married with two children of his own. Martha lived in her own residence with two male children.

Five of John and Martha's children moved to northern Kentucky. Thomas would marry Roxanna Odell (born June 2, 1812 in Maine) in Cincinnati, Ohio on October 24, 1830. Thomas and Roxanne resided in Ohio for a period of time before moving to Kentucky. They had 11 children. Two of their children were born in Cincinnati. Theodore was born June 30, 1832, and Quincy was born July 3, 1834. Four of the children were born in Burlington, Kentucky. Eliza was born August 10, 1836; Martha Zane was born March 8, 1838; Thomas Zane was born January 21, 1840 and died on February 8, 1842; and John Odell Roberts was born September 17, 1843. Five of their children were born at Middle Creek Mills, Boone County, Kentucky. Roxanna was born February 10, 1846; Mary was born January 7, 1849; the second Thomas Zane was born October 4, 1851; Isabella was born December 7, 1853; and Julia Ella was born July 21, 1856. [23]

Benjamin Roberts married Lucinda E. Smith (born May

10, 1810 in Indiana). Reverend G.R. Jones married them on January 12, 1832 in Butler County, Ohio. Ben owned many parcels of land in Rossville, Butler County, Ohio, what is now downtown Hamilton, Ohio. Ben moved to Carrollton, Kentucky in the mid 1840s and became a merchant. He operated a grocery store at the former post office building on Third Street. [24]

Ben and Lucinda had 10 children. Seven of their children were born in Ohio: Susanah (born in 1835), Amanda (1839), Ellen(1840), James (1841), Elenora (1842), Joseph (1843), and Martha (1845). Three of their children were born in Kentucky: Simeon (1847), Calvin (1852), and Alice (1856). Ben died on January 23, 1882 in Carroll County, Kentucky.

Very little is known about Simeon Zane Roberts. The 1860 Federal census shows him living in Carroll County, Kentucky with his sister Martha. He died on July 8, 1870 and is buried in the IOOF cemetery in Carroll County, Kentucky. His obituary in *The Carrollton Democrat* stated:

> Died at the residence of his brother Benjamin
> Roberts on Friday the 8 inst. S.Z. Roberts aged
> about 56 years. He was formerly known as a suc-
> cessful merchant at Prestonville but for some years
> past he has been a resident of Missouri.[25]

Dr. James M. Roberts married Anna Maria Symmes Harrison (born 1822) on October 4, 1839. The Boone County Clerk issued the marriage license. His brother Thomas signed as the binder on their marriage certificate.[26] The lineage of Anna is one of Boone County's most interesting. One of Boone County's first justices of the peace was a Revolutionary War veteran who came from New Jersey, Captain John Brown. He owned Sugar Grove Plantation, one of Boone County's finest farms at that time, which was located on the Ohio River. His plantation was across the Ohio River from the Harrison/Symmes estate. One can now stand at the Harrison monument in Ohio, located on the Harrison estate, and overlook the old Sugar Grove Plantation. One of

Captain Brown's children was named Clara. She married Zebulon Montgomery Pike. He was a brigadier general in the War of 1812 and the discoverer of Pikes Peak. His portrait hangs in the National Art Gallery in Washington, D.C. Zebulon and Clara had a daughter they named Clarissa. She married John Cleves Symmes Harrison, the oldest son of William Henry Harrison, who was elected President of the United States in 1840. The union of John Cleves Symmes Harrison and Clarissa Pike produced their daughter Anna Maria Symmes Harrison.[27]

Dr. James Madison Roberts and Anna Maria had two children, Gabrielle (born 1840) and James Montgomery (born 1844). Gabrielle died in 1846, and Anna Maria died in 1849. After his wife's death, James and his son moved in with his brother Thomas Roberts at his home in Middle Creek. James remarried on April 21, 1851 in Boone County to Martha A. Elliott.[28] They moved to Iowa, where they had two children, Clara (born 1858) and Edward (born 1851). James married a third time to Mary E. Marshall on May 27, 1869 in Missouri.[29]

Martha, the youngest child of John L. and Martha Zane Roberts, married Ira Collyer. His lineage is also distinguished. His father, Thomas Collyer, was a first lieutenant in the Somerset, New Jersey militia. He was under the immediate command of General George Washington. He was in the army for seven years, fighting in many historic Revolutionary War battles and suffering in the miserable winterquarters at Valley Forge in 1777-1778. At 73 years of age he moved to Nelson County, Kentucky. On December 23, 1815 he married Mary McAdams, of Bardstown, Kentucky, a locally renowned woman, who during an Indian attack on her life killed an Indian with an ax. On January 8, 1817, Ira was born.[30] The family moved to Hamilton, Butler County, Ohio. Ira was a member of the fire department in the City of Rossville/Hamilton.[31] Ira and Martha married on April 21, 1840. According to the 1820 Federal Census records, they were neighbors in Butler County. Ira lived in Liberty Township, and Martha lived in the town of Rossville. They were married by Reverend Charles W. Swain, the preacher for the Methodist Episcopal

Church for the Miami District, which included Cincinnati, Lawrenceburg, White Water, Mad River, Xenia, Piqua, Oxford and Hamilton. Martha and Ira moved to Carroll County, Kentucky in the mid 1840s, where Ira owned a dry goods store. Her mother, Martha Zane Roberts, moved in with them around 1850 and resided there until her death on August 20, 1870. In the summer of 1885 the family moved to become some of the most respected citizens of Marion, Kansas. On May 16, 1885 a newspaper reported:

> I.M. Collyer and son, Fred, left Tuesday for Marion Center, Kansas to which place Mr. Collyer expects to move his family about August 1. Mr. C has long been a resident of this county, a good deal of the time a prominent business man, and the many friends of himself and the family will regret to see them go. [32]

It was reported in Ira's obituary that Martha and Ira had 13 children, but information on only 12 of them can be found. [33] Six of the children were born in Ohio: The oldest of the children was Martha (d.o.b. 1841). Martha married James K. Pope of Boone County, and she died shortly thereafter on September 26, 1861. Their son Ira shows up in the census records living with the Collyers. He is believed to be counted among the 13 children. The other children born in Ohio are Mary (born 1844), Rebecca (1845), Carrie (1855), Ira (1857), and William (1862). The other six known children were born in Kentucky: Annabel (1848), Evaline (1849), John (1851), Joseph (1854), Edith (1864), and Frederick (1866).

When Thomas Roberts Senior and Roxanne Odell Roberts came to Boone County, they already had two children, Theodore and Quincy, who were born in Cincinnati. However, Quincy lived for only 12 days. Their third child, Eliza, was born in Burlington, but lived only 37 days. Martha, Thomas Zane and John also were born in Burlington (1838-1843). Thomas Zane lived barely two years. The remaining five children were born at "Middle Creek Mills." The inventor of the solar clock, Thomas Zane Roberts, was born on October 4, 1851. He was given the same name as the fifth child who had died nine years earlier.

When Thomas Roberts Sr. came to Burlington, he found a Boone County that had the following makeup of its population:

Population	10,034
Agriculture	3,019
Commerce	41
Manufacturers and Trades	322
Navigation	15
Learned Professions and Engineers	45
Learned Pensioners from Revolution or Military Service	18
Deaf and Dumb	9
Blind	5
Idiots	8
Academies and Grammar Schools	3
Scholars	8
Primary and Common Schools	4
Scholars	65
Number of White Persons Over 20 Who Cannot Read or Write	447[34]

Roberts came to Boone County as a carpenter. One of the senior Roberts' finest carpentry works still exists on East Bend Road, known as the Robert Chambers house. Built in the 1830s, it is considered one of the most spectacular Greek revival residences in Boone County and is listed in the National Register of Historic Places.[35] It took Roberts three years to complete his work. The carpentry work includes a self-supporting circular stairway, a unique semicircular door made to follow the concave line of the stairway hall, and many fine details in the interior finish.[36]

The exact date when the senior Roberts and Roxanne moved to Boone County is not known. The oldest child,

Theodore, was born in Cincinnati, Ohio on June 30, 1832 as was their second child, Quincy, who was born on July 3, 1834. Their third child, Eliza, was born on August 10, 1836 in Burlington, Kentucky. Martha (born March 18, 1838), the first Thomas Zane (January 21, 1840) and John Odell (September 17, 1843) were also born in Burlington. The Roberts family does not appear in the 1830 census for Boone County. The Robert Chambers house was built between 1832 and 1836. It is safe to conclude the Roberts family was living in Boone County in the early 1830s.

A review of the courthouse records shows that on July 26, 1845 Roberts purchased lot 73 of the Town of Burlington from Charles Chambers for $40. He sold it a few months later for $300 to William Perkins.[37] The records at the courthouse also show he took a mortgage to secure payment for carpenter work in 1842. One James M. Runyan was apparently in debt to several people in town. He owed merchants John Cave and Joseph Foster $300, John Riddell $300 for unsettled accounts, and Thomas Roberts $300.58 for carpenter work. Runyan gave a mortgage in favor of all of them secured by Lot 17 of the Town of Burlington (which was Runyan's home) as well as

> 3 beds and bedding and sheets, 2 bureaus, three tables, one Candle table, one candle stand, one writing desk, one large mantle clock, twelve chairs, two pair andirons, shovel and tongs, two looking glasses, lot of cupboard ware, tin safe, one cooking stove and all the fixtures thereunto belonging, one set of blacksmith tools.[38]

Roberts apparently was not paid by Runyan, and on April 7, 1851 he sold and assigned his note and mortgage to Milton Hamilton for $450.[39]

In 1846 the Roberts family moved to Middle Creek. Middle Creek was one of the earliest settlements in Boone County. John Tanner established the first settlement in Boone County in 1789 called Tanner's station (later Petersburg).[40] In 1790 brothers

James Ryle and John Ryle with their families, a sister (Mary Ryle, who later would marry Moses Scott) [41] and a slave came to Boone County from North Carolina following the Daniel Boone trail. They arrived at Tanner's fort, and while there Polly Ann Ryle was born to James Ryle and his wife, Sallie, on February 19, 1790. This was the first white child born in Boone County. In the spring of 1791 the Ryles left the fort and located near the mouth of Middle Creek. They contracted a fever and after two years decided to seek higher ground. They purchased land above the Middle Creek valley near Waterloo and Belleview from the government at a cost of 72 1/2 cents per acre.[42]

On January 9, 1846 Roberts purchased 257 acres of the Middle Creek valley from Jeremiah and Sophia Garnett. This tract contained the Garnett Mill. The deed describes the property as follows:

> "all that tract of land situated in Boone County State aforesaid on middle creek and commonly called the steam mill tract. . ."[43]

The purchase price was $3,500, and the Garnett's took a mortgage back for $3,000 payable in annual installments of $500. On November 11, 1848 Roberts sold an undivided one-half interest to his brother Ben Roberts for $1,925.[43] Many years later, on October 22, 1875, Thomas Roberts bought out brother Ben for the sum of $1,925 plus a three year note of $216 per year plus interest at 8 percent. [45]

By the year 1850, Roberts was farming 50 of the acres, and the farm had increased in value to $4,000. He owned 2 horses, 1 cow, 4 oxen, 2 cattle, and 100 swine. In 1849, his farm produced 100 bushels of wheat, 500 bushels of Indian corn, 10 bushels of Irish potatoes, and 300 pounds of butter. He slaughtered $95 worth of livestock. He also operated a water gristmill, producing 800 pounds of flour and 600 pounds of cornmeal. He cut and sold lumber in his mill. The raw logs were valued at $600. [46]

Roberts worked the farm with his family without the use of slaves. When Roberts came to Boone County, 21.8 percent of the county's population were slaves. By 1850 Boone County had 1,615 families and 982 farms. Approximately 30 percent of the families owned slaves, and 40 percent of the farmers owned slaves.[47] There is no record that Roberts or any of his family ever owned a slave. While most of the Middle Creek residents fought on the side of the Confederacy in the Civil War, sons John Odell Roberts and Theodore Roberts fought for the Union. Thomas Zane Roberts was too young to fight.[48]

Perhaps the best synopsis of the senior Thomas Roberts' life is contained in his obituary:

OBITUARY OF THOMAS ROBERTS
BOONE COUNTY RECORDER
Volume 2, No. 10
Nov. 30, 1876
** ** ** ** ** ** ** ** ** ** ** ** ** **

Obituary
Roberts—On the 23rd inst., after a lingering illness, Thomas Roberts, in the 71st year of his age.

The deceased came to Burlington about 1840, where he pursued his trade of house carpenter for a number of years, and then removed to the city of Covington, where he superintended the erection of many of the finer buildings of that day in that growing young city. In 1847 he became a partner and joint owner with John Riddell in the Middle Creek Mill property, and at the expiration of a year or two he bought out his partner and became sole owner of the premises till his decease. As a mechanic, the deceased was without a superior, in those branches of the business to which he had applied himself. He was said to be a thorough master of the science, as well as the practical part, of his art, and it was no unusual occurrence for his brother carpenters to resort to him for advice and assistance in the more scientific and finer parts of their work. From the time he became owner of the Middle Creek property to his death, he directed his attention to milling and farming. The deceased was of a quiet and retiring disposition. Never, on any occasion, did he force himself, or suffer himself to be put forward, to the occupancy of a leading or conspicuous position in society. He greatly preferred the quiet of his farm and home to the excitement and turmoil of public life. Hence it was that, possessed of good education, strong natural sense, a sound and discriminating judgment, a memory well stored with an abundance of information, acquired from an extensive and diligent reading of select authors, with keen perceptions and observations, a pure heart, and an honor above suspicion, he never filled a public office save that of Justice of the Peace, and this was forced upon him by his neighbors, who would accept of no refusal. Besides possessing the qualities of mind and heart that so well fitted the deceased for high public position and distinction, he was a kind neighbour, an indulgent father, and an exemplary Christian gentleman. He has gone from earth to that better land, but his example of a pure life, we trust, will not, can not, be without a good effect upon those he has left behind.[49]

* * * * *

Fellow members of the Grange passed the following resolution:
Tributary of Respect
The Hall of Belleview Grange, 634
Boone County, Kentucky, November, 1876.

WHEREAS, Our Divine Master above has removed from our midst, on the 23rd our beloved Brother,

Thomas Roberts, aged 71 years, whereby the community has lost one of its best citizens, the Church a devoted Christian, the Grange one of its brightest examples of a true Patron, his bereaved widow a kind husband, and his children a devoted father.

RESOLVED, that we tender our heartfelt sympathy to the bereaved family and friends, and that they be commended to him who hath said, "Write, Blessed are the dead which die in the Lord from henceforth; yea, saith the Spirit, that they may rest from their labors, and their works do follow them."

RESOLVED, that, as a token of respect to the memory of the deceased, the members of this Grange, wear the usual badge of mourning for thirty days.

RESOLVED, that a copy of these resolutions be sent to the family of the deceased, and a copy to the Cincinnati Grange Bulletin and Boone County Recorder for publication.

(R. H. Botts, James P. Kelley, J. M. Moody Committee).[50]

Many of those qualities of Thomas Roberts were passed on to his son and namesake, Thomas Zane Roberts.

The senior Thomas Roberts performed the carpentry work on the Chambers house in the 1830s. It has been called "one of the most spectacular Greek Revival residences in Boone County" and "the elaborate north doorway represents the most academically correct use of the relatively sophisticated Greek Doric Order in Boone County." (Images of America: Burlington, p. 75)

One of the best examples of Roberts' handiwork in the Chambers house is the circular stairway. The stairway seems to hang in mid-air. The door in the background is curved to fit with the rounded wall.

Thomas Roberts built this house in the 1830s for Robert Huey, one of the largest landowners and slaveholders in Boone County. The circular stairway and front door entrance are remarkably similar to the Chambers house. Greg and Linda Salsbury presently own the house.

CHAPTER THREE

T. Z.

Thomas Zane Roberts was born on the Middle Creek farm and lived there his entire life. Josephine Cason wrote the following about Roberts:

> When he was a little boy growing up he went with his sisters to Sunday School at the old Middle Creek Church. But when about ten to twelve years of age the other boys would come every Sunday and coax him to go swimming or fishing in the creek. The girls wanted him to go with them to Sunday School, and he would always have stubbed toes or stone bruises on his heels and would not go, so his mother would have to take charge. [1]

Apparently his parents must have taken charge as God and religion became and remained an important part of his life. Roberts united with the Middle Creek Baptist Church at age 16. That same year he became an instructor for Sunday school classes, a post he occupied for over 50 years. His father taught him carpentry, farming and milling, which Roberts did throughout his life. His parents also impressed upon Roberts the importance of education.

During his life Roberts would establish himself as a carpenter, miller, teacher, singer, musician, horologist, astronomer, poet, author, painter, inventor, stonemason and surveyor. His boundless energy was with him from a very young age. Josephine Cason wrote, "He was never idle very much in his younger life."[2] A reading of his diary and reviewing his accomplishments would certainly make that an understatement.

Roberts' diary shows him to be a very social person. He constantly traveled around the county, staying with friends and being away from home on many occasions for days at a time. He made time for social events and very often created the opportunities himself. He was said to be competent with several musical instruments, including the organ, flute, and violin. The latter two instruments he made himself. He was an accomplished singer. His sisters and brothers were also excellent singers. He was a member of the Middle Creek/Belleview Baptist Choir, as well as song leader and organist. He taught singing schools. It was said he always carried a tuning fork with him.[3] He organized his own social gatherings into what he called "sings." An example of his attendance at sings is as follows:

Sings

January 1882
9 to 13 Teach – to also on Wednesday night to a sing
at John Tanner's on Friday eve. To see Dixon
to a musical
16 to 20 Teach – Wednesday eve went to a Sing at
Jeff Carpenters – on Friday eve go to a sing
at Mr. Howe
21 Dan, Jimmy and I go to a Speaking at Union
22 . . . to a sing at Mrs. Boothes

Feb
3 to a play at Tom Rice
5 to a sing at Mrs. Boothes
11 to a sing at John Tanners
12 Mr. Dobbins had a sing today
28 to a sing at Mrs. Boothes

He attended parties and described in his diary one particular party at age 26 as "a wild time". He attended plays, one of which is dealt humorously in his narrative story contained in his published work *Lively Stories for Lively Folks: Second Paper.* Speeches, debates and lectures were always of interest to him. Roberts was a man of temperance and did not believe in drinking alcohol. Temperance was a movement of moral reform appearing amid the aftermath of the Civil War. In February 1869 Covington held a celebration to honor the pledging to total abstinence of 1,000 veteran dram drinkers.[4] Roberts would travel significant distances to hear a temperance lecture.

While Roberts enjoyed the social life, his dedication and love of God is clearly evident throughout his life. The famous Boone County pastor Robert Kirtley wanted to send the 19- year-old Roberts to Georgetown College to be educated in the ministry, but Roberts' father wanted him to remain on the farm.[5]

Religion permeated his entire life. He always attended church on Sundays, sometimes two different churches in the same day. This would be an endurance test as travel was generally by horseback. There was a scarcity of ministers, and not every church had services every week. This 1875 article from the *Boone County Recorder* shows the challenges for a person who wanted to attend a church every Sunday.

CHURCH MEETINGS

Lutheran Church at Hebron; Rev. W. C. Barnett, Pastor. Services held the first and third Sundays in every month.

Lutheran Church in Hopeful; Rev. W. C. Barnett, Pastor. Services held the second and fourth Sundays in every month.

Baptist Church at Big Bone; Rev. J. A. Kirtley, Pastor. Service held every fourth Saturday.

Baptist Church at Burlington; Rev. J. A. Kirtley, Pastor. Services held on the third Saturday in every month.

Christian Church at Florence; Rev. W. S.

Keene, Pastor. Services the first Sunday in every month.

Christian Church at Point Pleasant; Rev. W. S. Keene, Pastor. Services on the third Sunday in every month.

Christian Church at Constance; Rev. H. J. Foster, Pastor. Services held the second Sunday in each month.

Universalist Church at Burlington; Rev. J. S. Cantwell, Pastor. Services held on the fourth Sunday in every month.

Baptist Church at Bullitsburg; Rev. J. A. Kirtley, Pastor. Services held the first Saturday in every month.

Baptist Church at Middle Creek; Rev. R. E. Kirtley, Pastor. Services on the second Saturday in every month.

Christian Church at Petersburg; Rev. W. S. Keene, Pastor. Services held on the second and fourth Sundays in every month.

Christian Church at South Fork; Rev. H. J. Foster, Pastor. Services held the third Saturday in every month.

M. E. Church at Burlington; Rev. Benj. F. Orr, Pastor. Services held the first Sunday in every month.

Presbyterian Church at Burlington; Rev. Dr. J. W. Hall, Pastor. Services held on the second Sunday in every month.

Baptist Church at Sand Run; Rev. R. E. Kirtley, Pastor. Services held on the fourth Saturday in every month.

Baptist Church at East Bend; Rev. C. S. Carter, Pastor. Services held on the third Saturday in every month.

Baptist Church at Florence; Rev. Geo.

Varden, Pastor. Services held on the second
Saturday in every month.

Baptist Church at Mt. Pleasant; Rev.
Benjamin Lampton, Pastor. Services held on the
second Saturday and Sunday in each month.

M. E. Church at Petersburg; Rev. D. H.
Marimon, Pastor. Preaching first and third Sundays
and Saturday night previous.

M. E. Church at East Bend; Rev. D. H.
Marimon, Pastor. Preaching second and fourth
Sunday and Saturday night previous.[6]

Roberts would attend revivals or Sabbath conventions
night after night. Prayers are expressed numerous times throughout Roberts' diary. Roberts was a poet, and some of his poems had
religious themes. Above the fireplace in his house he carved GOD.
When he worked on the construction of the church at Belleview,
when it moved from Middle Creek, he carved the words JESUS
SAVES on an arch about the dais.

Roberts served the Middle Creek Baptist Church and the
religious community in Boone County throughout his life. He
taught Sunday school for over 50 years. He was elected superintendent of Sabbath Schools for Boone County. He served as clerk
of the Belleview Baptist Church, the successor to Middle Creek
Church. He was a speaker at Sabbath School conventions, even
serving as chairman. He wrote articles about his faith. One well-
received speech was "How I Study My Sunday-School Lesson." He
read and studied the Bible every day. He was selected to be a dea-
con but disqualified himself on scriptural principles because he
never married.[7]

One reason why Roberts was perhaps so active is that he
never married. He remained a bachelor his entire life. It wasn't
because he wasn't interested in the girls. Josephine Cason wrote,
"When a boy he was a mischievous boy like most other boys
always teasing and playing pranks on the girls."[8] She also wrote,
"He like other young men liked the girls and had all the reverence

and respect for the women though he was never married."[9]

Roberts probably had little trouble finding social companionship. He stood 5 feet 8 inches tall and weighed about 155 pounds. He had dark black hair and a full beard. He kept his beard his entire life.[10]

It appears somewhere in his 20s Roberts became more serious about developing a relationship with women. On December 8, 1879 Roberts went to Sunday School and then to visit at J.F. Ryle and afterwards to Len Clore's. His diary thereafter is replete with visits to either the Ryle's or Clore's. Due to the difficulty of travel it was not unusual for Roberts to stay the night as their guest. On January 30, 1880 he went to see Ella Ryle on her last day of school at the Beech Grove schoolhouse where she was the schoolteacher. He apparently took her home to her parents' house and spent the night. He must have had some feelings for Ella. In his father's justice of the peace book Roberts generally wrote in pencil or black pen. However, numerous times in the front of the book, in beautiful handwriting in bright blue ink he wrote the name "Ella N. Ryle." The only other time he used blue ink was when he wrote his own name, "T. Z. Roberts." Also interesting is an undated newspaper article pasted in the justice of the peace book. It states:

> Had a sing at the Universalist Church, Sunday evening. The exercises were conducted satisfactorily by Prof. Roberts and Miss Ella Ryle. They (Tom and Ella) left the church together, and went down the road humming Old Hundred-happy hearts

A search of the *Boone County Recorder* shows this is a newspaper article that had been cut out from the Waterloo neighborhood news section and reported on May 17, 1877.[11] Also interesting is that on the same page of his writing in the justice of the peace book he wrote:

Dec. 8, 1879
First Time

That is the day he went to both the Ryle home and the Clore house.

On February 8, 1880 Roberts wrote in his diary:

What this means only Roberts knows. It is believed that N throughout his diary referred to Nora Clore.

On April 11, 1880 Roberts wrote in his diary:

> Go to Ch. with N go to J Kites also to Jonas Clore's, take N home.

The diary entry does not tell us this, but we find out later in his diary this is the day he proposed marriage to Nora Clore. A newspaper article in the *Boone County Recorder* does indicate the engagement. The Waterloo news correspondent reported the following on May 6, 1880:

> Considerable interest is being manifested by the denizens of our little villa in behalf of our friend, T.Z.R., who has not been seen for a fortnight. We fear he is a pilgrim in some foreign land.
> We congratulate you on being nominated for the office of Circuit Clerk, but one thing lackest thou yet, and if you engage two "on 'em" I need the one.[12]

Right above the April 11, 1880 diary entry he wrote:

> Oh Thou who hearest prayer. bless all for whom I should pray with all heeded blessings—and at last save them in heaven.

He spent a lot of his time with Nora thereafter until July 31, 1881, when he wrote in his diary:

Went to SS-also to Jas. J. Ryle's also to Mr. Dick
Clements-Take Nora Clore home and QUIT.
Forever
We have been engaged since April 11, 1880 but she
is not true to me, and I told her today that I would
not come again as a lover and shall not.

On September 14, 1881 he wrote that he went to
Belleview "after my Ring."

Thereafter it appears he began dating a girl by the name of
Maggie Marshall. On July 10, 1881, 21 days before he broke up
with Nora, he noted that he, Nora and Maggie went to Church
together. The next month in his diary he wrote:

> August 25: Go to Teacher's Institute. Pass
> the night at John's.
> August 26: Go Institute also to John J.
> Marshall's to arrange matters.

On October 30 he notes he went to church with Maggie.
On December 24 he walked all the way to Belleview to see
Maggie. He wrote ,"Maggie Marshall and I get on the boat and go
to Ghent and spend very pleasant Christmas at Henry Wises." On
December 25 he wrote, "very pleasant Christmas at Henry Wise."
On December 26 and 27 he wrote "Fun alive." He didn't return
home on the boat until December 30 . He concluded these entries
with the following prayer:

> The Lord has followed me with a multitude of bless-
> ings through the past year. Blessings and praise be
> my hearts offering all the years of my life to my
> Friend in heaven.

In September of 1882 he went to the Clores' although he
notes it was "by invitation." In February of 1883 he notes he "went
to Len Clore's to take N to Abs Aylor." There are periodic refer-

ences after that date of going to Nora's house. An interesting note is made on April 8, 1883 when Roberts writes: "Start to J.T. Ryles but Len Clore stops me." He doesn't say why Nora's father stopped him or what he had to say. As Len Clore was the city marshall of Waterloo, undoubtedly Roberts did stop. He did start visiting the Clores' again on a periodic basis. "N" no longer appeared in his diary, but several weeks after Len Clore stopped Roberts he wrote, "to church in evening then home with Nora Clore." Also during these years after the breakup with Nora, Roberts still saw Maggie Marshall. The last mention of Maggie occurred on July 26, 1885. He wrote in code in his diary just a few weeks earlier on July 5, 1885:

Then on September 20, 1885 he wrote in code in his diary, as he did on two previous occasions when referring to Nora:

Two weeks later he wrote in code in his diary again after being at Henry Clore's:

This was written on October 4, 1885 on his 34th birthday. After that he never mentioned Nora or Maggie again. There is no indication he ever dated again.

With respect to his feelings, Roberts was a very private person. He rarely expressed in his diary how he felt about any of the persons in his life. What women he did feel something special for he expressed it in a code that only he could read. In his diary he wrote in code only four times. However, in his justice of the peace book he did so many more times. It also appears that on many occasions he would write what he did on a day in the justice of the peace book and later rewrite it in his diary. That is probably why the final draft in his diary is always in such fine handwriting. A comparison between the justice of the peace book and his diary shows that he wrote much more often in code than the four times reflected in his diary. There are changes between his original drafts and final drafts that are quite interesting. Some of the notes from his original drafts are scratched through, and we are only told in his final diary that he was with this girl or that girl that day. Many of the pages of the justice of the peace book are simply torn out.

The earliest time Roberts used code was on May 3, 1879. The entry in the justice of the peace book is:

When it was written in the final diary it was written as "Go to theatrical at Burlington with Fanny R." [Rice]

Later that same month he used the code again in the justice of the peace book on May 25, 1879:

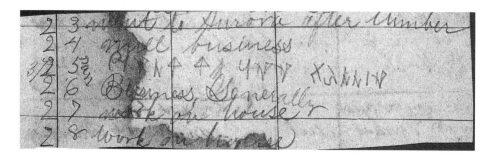

The writing for the same date in his dairy is as follows:

> Go to M. S. Rices

The interesting thing about Fanny Rice is that on September 1, 1878 Roberts wrote he "gave Fanny sketch". Josephine Cason wrote that Roberts was an artist and drew pictures of girls he liked.

The year 1880 shows he wrote in code in the justice of the peace book many more times than the one time in his diary. The only time the code appears in his diary in 1880 is on February 8. This is the day after he had been to the Rice's and seven days before he went to the Marshal's and the same day took Nora Clore to church. It is truly interesting to compare the entries for February 15, 1880:

Justice of the Peace book:

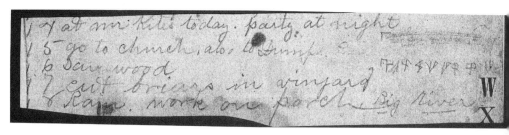

Diary

Go to ch. Also to J. T. Marshalls. also to Ch with Nora Clore.

More code appears in the Justice of the Peace book a week later on February 22, 1880.

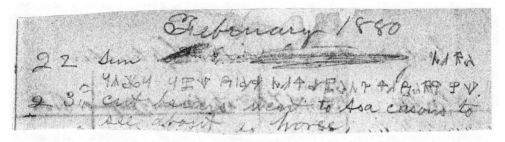

The corresponding diary entry states: "At Mr. Clores today."

A few weeks later in his diary he wrote on March 21, 1880, "Go to Mr. Clores," but his writings in the justice of the peace book for that day are partly scratched through and the rest is written in code:

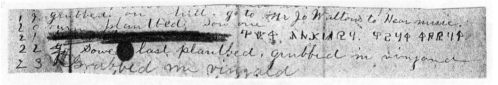

The intrigue continues throughout the year. On May 1, 1880 he wrote in code the following:

The diary replaces it with the single letter "O."

Twice in July in the justice of the peace book he scratched over writings and replaced them with "Go to ch-also to L.C.s" [Len Clore] and on the other occasion wrote, "Miscellaneous and C." He does it again on August 21, 1880. He scratches out four lines in the Justice of the Peace book and replaces them in the diary with simply "Go to ch with N".

The most interesting of all is the August 28 and 29, 1880 comparisons.

> Diary: 28   Go to Rising Sun – stop at Len C's
> Go to the Dock's P.T.N.
> Take N to Ust. Church

The justice of the peace book entry states:

28:    Go to Rising Sun, stop at Mr. C's, go to Docks
29:    Go to Universalist Ch. with
    Nora Schlechten ? mertz

What does this mean? Was this a "pet" name? A real name? Several German scholars who have reviewed the writing believe it is meant to read "schlechten schmertz" meaning "terrible pain," which would indicate the problems they were having in their relationship at this time. One thing that is clear is Roberts revealed more in his writings in the justice of the peace book before he rewrote the entries in his diary. Mystery remains because many of the pages in the justice of the peace book have been torn out.

One of the people who knew Roberts best, Josephine Cason, wrote:

> He like other young men, liked the girls and had all reverence and respect for the women, though he never married. They say at the age of 23 he learned to think a lot of a lovely girl and he drew a picture of her as he was also an artist and could do this easily and he put this picture in a strong box with her letters and kept it with several other girls, but from some cause or causes he remained a bachelor. I also have a painting he made of himself talking to a girl and a sunset scene and there are some other drawings."[13]

Ruth Kelly relates she spoke to Roberts about never marrying. She stated Roberts would simply say that he felt there was somebody intended for everybody. He further said if that was the case he guessed his intended died in infancy with the whooping cough. That was the only thing she ever heard Roberts speak about romance.[14]

Although still a young man at 34, and even though he lived for another 40 years, there are no further clues thereafter about his relationships.

This is the only known picture of T.Z. Roberts without a beard, taken when he was 22 years old.
He is posing with his sisters Belle and Ella.

Self-portrait of T.Z. Roberts.

The above is a draft of a drawing Roberts did of himself laying against the tree in front of his house. It was drawn on the front page of an 1870 edition of the Webster Dictionary. A final drawing was drawn in the front of the Roberts family bible, but the bible has been lost since Ralph Cason's death.

CHAPTER FOUR

MIDDLE CREEK BAPTIST CHURCH

When the Roberts family came to Middle Creek, the area already had its own church. This church would become and remain a large influence in Thomas Zane Roberts' life. The Baptist Church was established in Boone County in 1794 at Bullittsburg. Members of this Church would establish the Middle Creek Church in 1803. Members of the Middle Creek Church would establish the East Bend Baptist Church in 1819, establish the Baptist Church in Burlington in 1842 and establish the Big Bone Baptist Church in 1843.

In 1803 about 20 members of the Bullittsburg Baptist Church petitioned the church to constitute them as a new church in Middle Creek.[1] Bullittsburg is said to be the first town mapped out in Boone County by Cave Johnson in 1796.[2] It was a long way for the people of Middle Creek to travel to Bullittsburg in those days. The Bullittsburg Church minutes of March 5, 1803 stated:

> A request for some of the members at the south end of this Church for helps to assist them in forming a constitution, if to them it should be expedient, we therefore appoint Brethren DeWeese, Cave Watts, Matthews, Kirtley, Hall and Webb as helps to meet at the new meeting house by brother Sebree's next Saturday for that purpose.

The church was initially named "The Church of Christ at Middle Creek."[3] It was truly a Baptist denomination and later became known as simply "The Middle Creek Baptist Church."

The constituting members of the Church were as follows:

Christopher Wilson	Lucy Wilson
William Brady	Heatha Brady
Uriel Sebree	Fanny Sebree
Jamison Hawkins	Ruth Hawkins
William Rogers	Sally Rogers
Elijah Hogan	Lucy Hogan
Isaac Carlton	Dorcas Carlton
Thomas Carter	Nancy Carter
John Ryle	Elizabeth Ryle
James Ryle	Sally Ryle
Anthony (slave)	Mildred Sebree
Alice (Slave)[4]	

The first official church meeting was held on April 16, 1803. Moses Scott, one of the founding fathers of Boone County and the first county surveyor, was elected the first clerk of the church.

The first church building was a log cabin on the Uriel Sebree property, close to the Roberts farm. The exact location is not certain as according to church records Mr. Sebree was to convey to the church two acres of land with the church meeting house on it, but no deed was ever recorded.[5] A plaque now stands on the east side of Middle Creek road on or about the place the log cabin church stood.

The congregation grew, and on March 4, 1812 the members of the church passed a motion to build a new church building. A meeting was held at the home of William Garnett, who served as pastor from 1812 to 1825. The congregation decided to build the church on a high ridge overlooking the Middle Creek valley. John J. Marshall donated 21/4 acres upon which land the church was built.

The new church was a frame building built on a stone foundation. It was 28 x 20 feet. The minutes show the church trustees were to raze the old building along Middle Creek Road and to sell any salvageable materials to help defray the cost of the new church building. The first services were held in the new building in November of 1813, although it wasn't completed until September of 1814. In 1818, a revival year, 93 people were baptized in the waters of Middle Creek, and 10 were received by letter. This increased the church membership from 55 to 158.[6] Fourteen members of the church were dismissed in 1819 to constitute a church at East Bend.[7]

The first stove was installed in the church in January of 1822 at a cost of $42.68¾. In 1829 the clerk, Moses Scott, reported that church services had become so crowded that at times the building could physically hold only half of those attending the services. Therefore, a resolution was passed in August of 1829 to appoint a committee to study building a new meeting house or enlarging the existing one. The committee reported back the following month. It was decided to build a new building on the same site. It was to measure 34 x 50 feet. The goal was to have the new church built by August 1830. It was built and described as "a good substantial building but badly arranged."[8]

In June of 1846 this building underwent substantial repairs that were not finished until May of 1847. Excavation at the site has produced two types of brick, suggesting one type probably was produced at the site and the other was a more manufactured type. This suggests that construction during the years 1830 and 1847 both were of brick.

Twenty one members of the church left in 1842 to constitute a new church in Burlington.[9] The next year 44 members left to form a new church at Big Bone.[10] In 1862 the Middle Creek Church hosted the North Bend Association of Baptist Churches. In 1866 the church started its first Sunday School program. At Sunday School the students were taught the Bible but were also taught simple education – reading, writing, arithmetic and singings.

Roberts wrote in his diary that he "joined" the church in May of 1868 at the age of 16. He had attended church with his family as a young child, so the entry in his diary probably refers to his decision to be baptized. In fact, the church minutes of Saturday

May 9, 1868 reflect the following:

Middle Creek Church Record
Book 2ND

At a meeting held by the Church at Middle
Creek Sat. May 9th, 1868 –
R. E. Kirtley Mod. –

The reference respecting Bro. Robert Rice
was taken up. The Committee appointed to see Bro.
reported that they had attended to the order of the
Church as regards that matter, and that Bro. Rice
still persisted in being released from the Church the
report received and the Committee discharged –
Bro. Rice not being present to give satisfaction, he
was by a vote of the Church excluded

Received by experience for baptism John
Roberts, Thomas Roberts, Anna Roberts, Mary
Roberts, Jno. J. Marshall.

Adj. – S.P. Brady Cl.

He taught Sunday School shortly thereafter, something he
did almost his entire life. The third entry in his diary states:
"Attended Sabbath School Convention at Middle Creek Church."
Sabbath School was not held at the church but at the Locust Grove
Schoolhouse until 1915, when it was moved to the Beech Grove
Schoolhouse. Roberts served as Sunday School superintendent
from 1895 to 1903.

When Roberts "joined" the Middle Creek Baptist Church
in 1868, the church was in a monumental decision-making
process. The building again was in need of repair. A committee was
appointed to look into effecting repairs or building a new church.
Michael Clore offered to donate a building lot for a new church

building in Belleview. The church decided not to move. A major component to the decision was the congregation didn't raise enough commitment to make the necessary capital improvements. Nothing was done. In 1874 the spring near the church that had always served as its source of water dried up. A cistern was dug and a pump was installed. In June of 1876 a severe thunderstorm seriously damaged the church. S.P. Brady, a former church clerk, who wrote a history of the church, called it a "baby cyclone." *The Daily Recorder*, a former daily Boone County newspaper, reported the church building was destroyed by cyclone.[11] *The Boone County Recorder* reported:

> The following results of the wind storm on last Friday have been reported to us: The roof was taken off The Middle Creek Baptist Church, the gable ends blown down and the building otherwise considerably damaged. The roof was new, not being more than a year or two.[12]

On October 28, 1876 the *Boone County Recorder* reported:

> The Middle Creek Church still remains the mass of ruins to which it was rendered by the storm. The rebuilding seems abandoned. There is some disagreement as to…where it should be located.[13]

In the meantime church services were held at the Locust Grove Schoolhouse.

In the early years of Boone County, travel was by foot or horseback. The first personal horsedrawn buggy was brought to Boone County by Ed Fowler on a return trip from South Carolina in 1826.[14] The first stage coach line was established through Boone County in 1818 by Abner Gaines.[15] The first railroad built through Boone County was in 1869.[16] Middle Creek Church on the ridge could be reached only by foot or horseback.[17] By the 1870s the horse and buggy was becoming a more preferred way of travel in the county than walking or by horseback. S. P. Brady , who wrote *History of Middle Creek Baptist Church* in 1874, provided this thought:

> It will be remembered that the old meeting house was located in one of the most inaccessible places in the whole vicinity. In the early days when the first little log hut was built here this did not matter as people did not go to meeting in those days in buggys but either walked or rode on horseback. But when the last call was extended to Bro. Kirtley the conditions were changing. The era of saddles was giving way to the era of carriages; and Bro. Kirtley, being a farseeing man, recognized the necessity of removing the house of worship to a place more accessible…[18]

In 1877 the church congregation decided to build a new church in the river bottoms, known as Belleview. This area is still referred to as "Belleview Bottoms." This Ohio River town was established in 1815 and underwent several name changes. When a post office was established there it was designated the name of "Grant." For some period of time the name was spelled as Bellevue. In the late 1880s the spelling was changed from Bellevue to Belleview.

The choice of Belleview as a church site is easy to understand. It was easy to travel to and not too far from the Middle Creek church site. It was on the turnpike to the county seat of Burlington and located on the river. This is about three miles from the old church site using modern roads and is only one mile as the crow flies.

In September of 1877 the church deacons were ordered to "sell off so much of the land belonging to Middle Creek Church as is not occupied as a graveyard at the old location and hand the proceeds over to the building committee to assist in building a new house."[19]

In December of 1877, the Boone County clerk's records show five acres of the Middle Creek Church property was sold to

James Bruce for $43.68.[20] T. Z. Roberts purchased one acre 30 poles from the church on December 3, 1877 for $35.62.[21]

The new church at Belleview was dedicated in February of 1878. The church continued to call itself the "Middle Creek Church of Bellevue." However, on September 12, 1885 the congregation decided to cut the ties to Middle Creek when it passed the following resolution:

> Whereas, the church at its last meeting dropped the name "Middle Creek" and adopted "Bellevue" instead, on motion T.H. Sutton was appointed to have the like changed in the County Clerk's office at Burlington.[22]

While there was no longer a church on Middle Creek, religion remained the most important driving force of Roberts' life. He studied the Bible daily.[23] He attended church every Sunday of his adult life except one, which motivated him to build his first clock. He attended church sometimes twice in a day, and there are periods in his diary where he attended church every day for a week, not an undaunting task considering travel in those days. His diary is replete with prayers of his innermost feelings. Some examples:

June 30, 1873	Remember thy Creator in the days of thy youth
October 31, 1875	Do thou, Oh Lord visit me in loving kindness and guide me aright. Forgive my sins.
August 30, 1876	How I have failed to do thy will. O God forgive me and guide me aright.
November 30, 1877	Lord I desire to thank thee for Thy continued mercies and blessings
March 31, 1880	Oh Thou who hearest prayer. Bless all for whom I should

	pray with all heeded bless ings—and at last save them in heaven.
October 30, 1882	Oh, Thou who art Divine. Praise—honor and glory to Thy great name forever.
February 28, 1883	How wondrous art Thou O Lord God in all thy works. In wisdom hast Thou made them all. Thou doest all things well.
October 31, 1883	Lord God in heaven, have mercy on me and forgive my sins.
March 31, 1884	Mighty Redeemer God Above Let me forever Rest in Thy Love
December 31, 1887	Lord Jesus how much I have to thank Thee for.
June 30, 1888	Lord Jesus, Thou hast been merciful to me beyond compare.
August 31, 1890	My Lord and Saviour Jesus Christ. How great is Thy love and mercy towards me, a sinner. Praise to THEE forever.
March 31, 1891	Create within me a clean heart and lead me in right paths, oh my God.
November 30, 1892	Lord Jesus, I confess my sins and wickedness before Thee, but I am Thy servant. Help me to do Thy will. Pardon and save me I implore.

Roberts certainly gave his time in service to his church. He served as church clerk, Sunday School superintendent, treasurer of the cemetery fund, trustee, Sunday School teacher, organist and song leader. When the congregation decided to undergo an enlargement and repair the church in 1903, Roberts assisted with his master carpenter skills in building the church in Belleview. No doubt the Middle Creek Baptist Church was an important force in Roberts' life and he in it.

PROGRAMME OF THE

Sunday-School Convention,

TO BE HELD WITH

BIG BONE BAPTIST CHURCH,

July 28 & 29, 1888.

Introductory Sermon—

A. C. Davidson.

Organizing Convention.

Essay—Is the Sunday-school a part of our church work? —J. H. Averill.

Discussion by   R. E. Kirtley.

Essay—Is it the duty of all our members to engage in S. School work as a means of growth in grace and knowledge?—   J. H. Butler.

Discussion by   Dr. S. M. Adams.

Essay — Should Distinctive Baptist Principles be taught in our Sunday-Schools?—   T. L. Utz.

Discussion by   J. A. Kirtley.

Essay — Our Sunday-School Literature.   J. H. Fullilove.

Discussion by   C. H. Green.

Essay—Probable effect of Sunday-School work in Experimental Religion.   Z. T. Roberts.

Discussion by   Dr. D. M. Bagby.

Essay—Importance of Cooperation between Teachers and Superintendent.

Andrew Ellis.

Discussion by   A. L. Vickers.

Boone County Recorder
Vol. XIII No. 35
July 4, 1888
Page 3

This picture of Middle Creek is below the hill where the Old Middle Creek Baptist Church stood. Many people received their baptism in Middle Creek. Ninety-three people were baptized in 1818, a revival year. The Boone County Recorder reported that the Belleview Baptist Church baptized 56 people in Middle Creek more than 100 years later in November 1919.

Thomas Zane Roberts

The picture above shows where old Middle Creek Road left present Middle Creek Road and ran through Middle Creek itself.

The picture above shows old Middle Creek Road as it approaches the old Middle Creek Baptist Church site.

When the Middle Creek church was moved from its first location on Middle Creek Road to the top of the hill, the evidence shows construction at some point in time was of brick. Excavation shows there were two types of brick used. The brick on the top probably was made at the church site while the brick on the bottom is believed to have been made offsite.

CHAPTER FIVE

PROFESSOR ROBERTS

The formal amount of education that Roberts received is not exactly known. He was reputed to be an outstanding mathematician, orator and well read. The only thing Roberts ever wrote in his diary about his education was in the preamble "My first Teacher in school was Miss Wheatley."

The first school in Boone County was established in 1808 in North Bend Bottoms.[1] The next known school was in 1810 in East Bend, which is near Middle Creek.[2] In 1836 Kentucky established the Common School System. A survey of Boone County was done at that time, and 26 school districts were created.[3] The school term originally was three months, starting in September and ending before Christmas.[4] By 1881 Boone County had 41 schools with three- month terms and five schools with five-month terms.[5] A five-month term began in September and ended in February. It is obvious that the terms were meant not to conflict with the farming months. In 1881 Boone County also had 14 private schools and three academies.[6]

Roberts attended the common schools for his education. He attended a common school at Willoughby one winter, and the remainder of his common school experience was at Locust Grove. Undoubtedly, his education was supplemented by his parents, especially by his father who reportedly was

> possessed of a good education, strong natural sense, a sound and discriminating judgment, a memory well stored with an abundance of information, acquired from an extensive and diligent reading of select authors...[7]

T.Z. Roberts was described as "a home student and he read many, many books. He was a great reader."[8]

Roberts did attend the Morgan Academy in Burlington. This was the most noted academy in the area. It began in 1814 as the Burlington Seminary in 1820 changed its name to the Burlington Academy and also was known as the Boone Academy. Its name was changed in 1841 to the Morgan Academy after it was the recipient of the estate of Allen Morgan. A large brick building was built in 1857 to house the school.[9]

According to his diary, Roberts began at the Morgan Academy on December 8, 1873 at the age of 22 years. Josephine Cason wrote that he worked and saved up his money to attend. He stayed in Burlington with his older sister, Mary Craven, and her husband, Washington Craven. He finished the school term on March 13, 1874. What he took as courses can only be surmised. Advertisements by the Morgan Academy in the *Boone County Recorder* provide the following information:

Primary Department	8.00
Intermediate Department	12.00
High School Department	16.00[10]

A much earlier advertisement in the *Burlington Advertiser* newspaper reported :

Terms for Session of Five Months
For the Higher branches, Latin & c.,......$13.00
For Chemistry, Surveying & c.,............$10.00
For English, Grammar & c.,................$8.00
Primary Branches Education,..............$5.00
Extra charges for fuel, as heretofore

Tuition fees are lower than any other institution in the west.[11]

Roberts did not start his diary until his 21st birthday. He may have attended Morgan Academy at an earlier time before he started his diary. Josephine Cason wrote that Roberts "went a part of a term at the old Morgan Academy at Burlington and in playing ball he got badly hurt and was not able to go anymore for a long time…."[12] "Base-ball", as it was called then, was popular during this period. In fact, many people thought baseball was played too much. The first issue of the *Boone County Recorder* on September 23, 1875 stated "On the 11th inst. Burlington had 27 men playing base-ball. This certainly is base-ball to excess."[13] By 1913 Middle Creek sponsored its own team called the Middlecreek Allsorts.[14]

After finishing the Academy in 1874 Roberts returned to his father and mother's home. There he began his life as a farmer and miller. Roberts was not completely satisfied, as his education was put to little use. An opportunity arose the following year when the *Boone County Recorder* published its first issue. The proprietors, Riddell and Conner, announced in their maiden issue of September 23, 1875 that:

> anyone that wishes to embrace the opportunity of furnishing news from his sector will be supplied with stationery and a copy of the *Recorder* as long as he continues to write. We demand the true names of correspondents to accompany the communications, but will omit them from publication if preferred.[15]

Roberts accepted the invitation and began his brief career as a poet and writer. He did not use his name, but wrote under the pen name of "Zane." He kept copies of these writings pasted in his father's justice of the peace book. In that same book he pasted other articles on mathematical problems, astronomy, science, and poetry. How much of these writings in the justice of the peace book that were not published in the *Boone County Recorder* were his works or the works of others is difficult to determine. Those published in the *Boone County Recorder* had the words "written for the Recorder" on them. Others, such as those published in *Harper's Magazine* had his style but no proof he was the author. A review of those articles published in the *Boone County Recorder* does give an appreciation of his writing talents.

Roberts' first publication in the *Boone County Recorder* occurred on December 23, 1875. It was a poem entitled *Pensee*. It was a poem about Jesus' teaching on forgiveness. It was a fitting poem for his first publication as he truly was a man of God, a person who "read and studied the Bible every day" and "who knew it and could explain it,"[16] and already by this time had numerous years as a Sabbath School teacher. Even by this time he had already commenced the practice of writing prayers in his diary.

A few weeks later his second poem was published. *In the Depths* was a poem about memories and the importance of creating memories that brings us peace in our later years. He changed direction in his writings with his third poem, published two weeks later on January 27, 1876 and titled *Beware Boys*. In this poem he warns men about the misery brought about by marriage. His first narrative was published a little over a week later (February 6, 1876) titled *Queer, but Unquestionable*. This was a short story about courtship and love. On February 6, 1876 he published the poem *Profanity* in which he urged the readers not to swear if they wished to gain heaven upon their death. Less than three weeks later he published *Love,* a poem warning the readers to "go slow" in pursuing love. His second short story was published two weeks later titled *Lively Stories for Lively Folks First Paper,* a fictional story about a night of fishing. His next poem was published on May 4, called *Gracious Me*. He dedicated the poem to his friend, Charley Connor. His diary does reveal he had such a friend. This poem once again is about being in love with a "fair young girl." In the justice of the peace book where he pasted the poem is an article cut out of the newspaper (written by the editor) as follows:

> A certain young gentleman, who resides in a certain neighborhood not 100 miles from here, was meandering about the County Clerk's office last Saturday, and when we take into consideration his contribution to this issue, his maneuvers took the more suspicious.

Boone County Recorder
Vol 1 p 33
May 4, 1876

Underneath the article Roberts wrote "see the above" referring to the *Gracious Me* poem. *A Total Wreck* was published on May 11, 1876 following up on this article. The next month he published a poem about a mother who lost a child. The poem was "respectfully dedicated to my valued friend, Mrs. M.S. Rice." His diary shows he had been to their home on many occasions during this period of time, and on March 22, 1874 his diary indicates he attended the funeral of Maggie Rice.

Roberts published *Lively Stories for Lively Folks Second Paper* on June 29, 1876. It was a story about a party, and in the narrative he poked fun at a girl named Della. There was apparently an ongoing attack on this girl in the newspaper by Roberts as in *Gracious Me* and *A Total Wreck*. A week later Della retorted, publishing *Lookout Zane*, in which she lashes out at Zane in a poem for falsely proposing marriage to her in order to make fun of her. A week later Zane counters in his own poem titled *Poor Zane*, in which he states he is so hurt by Della's words that he shoots himself. The next month he publishes *Sensation of a Suicide*. His preamble to the editor describes it best:

> To the Editor of the Recorder:
> Sir—The following blank verse portrays the nervous phenomena attendant upon the reception of a good pistol ball, which passed through the right lobe of the cerebrum and out at the expansion of the skull over the volitive region, from the effects of which I am slowly recovering.
>
> > Your,
> > Zane[17]

Two months later on October 26, 1876 he publishes the poem *A Modern Husband*, a rather sad view of how some husbands mistreat their wife. This was his last published paper for the *Boone County Recorder.*

Shortly after he published his last poem Roberts' father died. This left Roberts at home as the person to take care of his mother. Roberts was 25 years old at the time. He had to turn his attention to more important matters, such as taking care of the family farm and milling business. These became fulltime occupations, but Roberts still found time for intellectual pursuits. Roberts still attended debates, lectures, plays or anything to stimulate the mind. During this period one of his favorite pursuits was attending the "spells." Similar to the modern day spelling bee, the spell was a contest between two teams of 15 members. Each common school usually had a team, with its professor as its coach, and the *Boone County Recorder* reported the contest took on a spirit of "fierceness" and "competitiveness."[18]

Roberts was a doer and not just a spectator. One example is that on November 22, 1876 he organized his own "literary society." These organizations were quite common during this period. Literary societies were organizations designed to engage their members in an intellectual atmosphere in which such things as debates, reading of essays or poems and sings would take place. Roberts' initial efforts at starting a literacy society were not immediately successful as this newspaper account reveals:

> A literary society was organized at the Locust Grove school house on last Thursday night. The weather being inclement, those who witnessed the society merge into existence were few. A programme was arranged for next Thursday night &c. The proposition for discussion is: "affirmed that a classical education is preferable to wealth." C.C. Conner and A.C. Kelly affirm and J.T. Marshall and T.Z. Roberts deny. The next meeting will be in part to permanently organize. Let the community around remember the night, and attend. Many pleasant and profitable hours can be spent in these society meetings.[19]

Unfortunately the next meeting did not bring much of a crowd, and its continued success was questionable. The newspaper account reported:

> The debating society organized at Locust Grove has as yet a glimmering existence. Will not both old and young, male and female, give it their support? There is nothing scarcely more improving, refining and enjoyable than a good literary society.[20]

The next meeting generated more interest, and the society appeared to be on its way:

> The literary society near here is gradually developing its muscle. It was "Ho! My comrades? see the signal," at the last meeting. Some reinforcements came in and manifested their intention to march along with it to victory.[21]

The literary society did become successful. A newspaper account of February 8, 1877 stated there was a large audience in attendance. Perhaps it was to hear the "musical department" sing its songs. More likely it was to hear a debate on whether "the education of woman should be as extensive as a man." Roberts served as a judge of that debate. It was decided in the negative.[22]

It was during this time that Roberts developed an interest in teaching. The annual Teachers Institute had begun in 1872. It was a gathering of county teachers in Burlington whose purpose was for the certifying of new teachers, examination of present teachers, and providing discussion and instruction for the purpose of improvement in the common schools of Boone County. The county school superintendent at the time would invite an outstanding educator from another area who would be designated as the conductor of the Institute and would preside over the week-long activities. In 1881 the teachers passed a resolution to request the School Committee to pass a levy on teachers at the Institute for purposes of procuring the services of professors to conduct the annual Institute.[23] There would be a wide range of subjects discussed. They included such subjects as primary reading, teacher preparation, language lessons, orthography, U.S. history, recitations, grammars and percentages, to name a few. A subject might be addressed by a teacher who had been selected in advance to prepare an essay for the occasion, or the subject might become the topic for a debate.

An example of an Institute's schedule is as follows:

Monday:	Organization of Institute; Reading; Spelling and Writing
Tuesday:	Primary and Advanced Grammar and Composition
Wednesday:	Civil Government and Geography
Thursday:	U.S. History; School Law and Theory and Practice
Friday:	Primary and Advanced Arithmetic, Physiology and Hygiene[24]

The Institute was not all work. Various choirs would entertain the members, or the local Terpsichorean Society would provide the entertainment. A guest speaker might be asked to speak or read an essay, or a local vocalist would perform. Roberts was part of the entertainment for the Teacher Institute on August 17, 1876. Roberts sang "tenor" as part of the Belleview choir that entertained the members of the Institute. Two years later Roberts would attend the Institute for purposes of being certified as a teacher.

Teaching seemed a natural pursuit for Roberts. He had an intense desire for knowledge. There was a financial aspect to teaching also. School terms were in the winter months, when Roberts was not farming or milling. It seemed perfect for Roberts. Roberts did in fact receive his teacher's certificate from the Teachers Institute. On August 16, 1878 he passed the first-class examination and received his certificate. In those days any person who passed the required examination could teach. Many of the teachers had not advanced beyond what is now grade eight in the elementary schools.[25]

Roberts immediately received a position at the same common school he had attended, Locust Grove. He began his first teaching job on September 16, 1878, and continued teaching for over 25 years. His first teaching position paid him $28 per month for five months or $140 per year. Drawing on a letter from the county superintendent published a month earlier on the allowance of funds, Roberts' classroom was probably composed of 16 pupils.[26] Boone County Schools were not separated into grades until shortly before the turn of the century. When Kentucky began its reorganization of schools around 1930, Boone County had 12 one-room schools, four two-room schools, two three-room schools, two consolidated schools, and five independent graded schools. The schools serving the Middle Creek area, which were Beech Grove, East Bend, Locust Grove, Willoughby and Woolper, all still were one-room schools.[27]

When Roberts began teaching there was not any established curriculum to follow or books to use. It was not until 1886 that a Teachers Association was created. One of its earliest orders of business was to pass a resolution instructing the county superintendent to "adopt a system of text books for use in our schools."[28]

The common school education certainly included the "3 R's" of reading, writing and arithmetic. The education bestowed beyond that was contingent upon the forté of the particular teacher. Roberts was a great mathematician, and his class would include a strong mixture of mathematics and geography. Upon numerous occasions over the years he benefited the members of the Teachers Institute with his knowledge of geography and mathematics. Since common schools only went to the eighth grade and the students had no high school to attend, Roberts would teach high school subjects to his more advanced pupils, particularly higher arithmetic and mathematics.

There was a difference of opinion as to whether the Bible should be used in the schools. The same Teacher's Institute where

Roberts received his first teaching certificate on August 16, 1878 published the following account:

> The last discussion of any importance was between J. W. Howe and Will Conner upon the use of the Bible in the schools. Howe favored the use of the Bible and Conner objected to it. They defended their respective positions with considerable skill, making the debate quite interesting to the several hearers.[29]

Roberts "read and studied the Bible every day and there wasn't many better Bible students anywhere around he knew it and could explain it."[30] It would be thought that Roberts taught the Bible to his public school classes.

However, Ruth Kelly, a former student of Roberts, stated this was not the case:

> Q.   Did he teach the Bible much? He was sup posed to have been really well versed in the Bible.
>
> A.   Well, no. Not per se, I wouldn't say. I think all of his teachings and all of Roberts' life reflected the great religious, deep religious feelings that he had. But he wasn't presumptuous about it. He never—he wouldn't have forced his religious beliefs on anybody or tried to have done it or have influenced you unlikely that way. But just the way he lived and the way he taught showed the deep religious belief he had.

Ruth Kelly further described Roberts' method of teaching:

He taught by the induction method. He never—if you asked him a question he never gave you the answer right off. He would talk with you about it and he would say—The one favorite saying of his was "Think for yourself. That's what your mind was given to you for." That made a great impression on me because that's what he really thought. He would talk to you about it or he would make leading remarks or ask you lengthy questions. If you couldn't come up with the answer then he would give you the answer. But he never told you anything until he was sure that you couldn't work it out for yourself.[31]

Roberts' second school term was at the Cason schoolhouse. It was located on land owned by his sister Belle and brother-in-law Ben Cason. The next year he taught on the other side of the county at Frogtown schoolhouse (October 3, 1881 to March 10, 1882). He stayed with the Dobbin family during the week and returned to his own home on the weekends. He was paid $180 for the term.

There is no record of Roberts teaching for the 1883 or 1884 school term. Several things happened during this period of time that could contribute to speculation as to why Roberts did not teach. He built his first clock. His eye was put out while chopping wood, causing him to be housed up for over a month and causing afflictions much longer. His marriage engagement with Nora Clore was broken off, and it is evident this had an emotional effect on him for quite some time.

On August 22, 1885 Roberts was back at the Teacher's Institute, and he was examined and was awarded a first class certificate. At the Institute he became one of the founders of the Teachers' Association:

> A committee consisting of J.C. Mack, L.L. Riley, T.Z. Roberts, Miss Lizzie Connor, and Miss Virginia Southgate was appointed to report upon the advisability of forming a County Teachers Association. The committee reported favorably, and in pursuance of their plan such an organization was formed with an enrollment of 29 teachers.[32]

Roberts returned to the Cason schoolhouse on October 21, 1885. He taught there for many years, and his name became synonymous with that school. Ralph Cason, the son of Ben and Belle Cason (Roberts' sister), received his education from Roberts at that school. He described Roberts as an excellent teacher, but a strict disciplinarian. He tells the following story:

> Uncle Tom's favorite form of punishment was a whipping. He'd tell the boy to go outside and get an "elm" switch. Then he would hit them on the back of their legs. Red marks would testify to the fact. One day at the school one kid told on a bigger boy for spitting paperwads. Uncle Tom took him and whipped him. Later that day the bigger boy came up and put his arm around the one who told and threw him to the ground behind the coal shed. He straddled him and just started punching. Then the boy got up, jumped the fence, and took for home. Uncle Tom told his brother to tell him to come back and take a whipping or he was expelled from school. The boy never did come back.[33]

Ruth Kelly's recollection of Roberts' discipline as a teacher:

> He called it his birch rod. He had a language all his own. He had that up on the wall. But I never saw it come down. I never saw him use it. But he referred to it as his birch rod. He expected everybody to behave properly and they did. They just did in those days. They did. He was a very strict disciplinarian, but he wasn't hard by nature or considered hard. I know I was sort of in awe of him.[34]

Compulsory school attendance did not exist at this time. A vote of the 1876 Teachers Institute showed that a majority of teachers was against making children attend school.[35] This didn't mean teachers weren't pushing for more education of children. Teacher D. M. Synder, who later became the superintendent of schools, wrote in the *Boone County Recorder* on March 16, 1876:

> "Therefore, I would say to all who are friends of the cause, and knowing at the same time that regularity in attendance is indispensable to a proper advancement, strive to remove this great detriment, and you will clearly see that much good has been done toward the building up of the noble cause of education, the true object of which is to make us wiser and better."[36]

The editor of the *Boone County Recorder* wrote the following article in favor of children attending school in 1878.

Absent from School.

There are hundreds of well-meaning but thoughtless county people who require their children to work on the farm when they ought to be in school, thus robbing them of the inestimable benefit of a good education. Two boys of the same age and ability start for school in May. One attends every day, rain or shine, during the term of four or five months, and is supplied with books according to his capabilities; the other comes one day and stays away two or three, and then possibly comes three or four more, coming and going like an intermittent fever. His excuses are often amusing, when we take into consideration the age and size of the little man. He has "had to help plant," or "log off a piece for potatoes," or "help ma," or "pick berries." His schooling averages about two days of the week. At the close of the term there is an examination. The first mentioned lad has made rapid progress in his studies. The foundation stone is laid for an intelligent, useful man. How is it with his companion? His advancement is scarcely perceptible. Who is to blame? Not the boy, and certainly not the teacher. Has the little farmer earned enough to pay for his lack of school culture? Emphatically, no! He has suffered an incalculable loss. Until a child has well entered his teens, he can be of little use on the farm. During childhood he should be allowed to attend school during ten months of the year. At fifteen the boy or girl is strong enough to be of use, while at the same time they will be capable of learning by practice and observation what they have learned only in theory, and many a lad or lass would lay up a fund of useful knowledge during the evenings and cold days, when otherwise unemployed, that would be a perpetual fountain of usefulness during all their lives. Whereas the child who has an occasional day, or week, or month at school, even from the time he is five years until he is twenty-one, will have a very limited amount of knowledge with which to begin a business life. And undoubtedly he will be obliged to knock about the world doing the drudgery of his former companions, looked upon as a sort of ignoramus incapable of using his best energies.[37]

There continued a debate in the county whether education was really important. The following is from another article published in the local newspaper:

Just a Question or Two.

IS YOUR SCHOOLHOUSE
AS UP TO DATE AS YOUR
NEW DAIRY BARN?
IS THE INTERIOR OF YOUR

SCHOOL AS MODERN AS THAT
NEW SILO?
   IS YOUR TEACHER AS COMPE-
TENT AS THAT TRAINER FOR
YOUR COLTS?
   IS THE SCHOOL AS WELL PAINT-
ED AS YOUR CHURCH?
   IS THE WATER AT THE SCHOOL
AS CONVENIENT AND AS GOOD
AS IT IS FOR THOSE YOUNG
STEERS?
   IS THE SCHOOLYARD AS BIG AS
THE PASTURE WHERE YOU EX-
ERCISE YOUR COLTS? [38]

Although Roberts' one-room schoolhouse would have been very "modest" and consisted of children of many different ages, there would have been no "negroes" or "mulattoes" in his school. While the Civil War may have ended slavery, there was no equality in the area of education. In the year following the Civil War the Kentucky General Assembly passed a law that negro schools should be supported by taxes on negro-owned property. On February 23, 1874 the Kentucky General Assembly passed "An Act to establish a uniform system of Common Schools for the colored children of the Commonwealth." Among its sections was a law making it unlawful to go to a school of the other race, and that in a rural county no colored school could be erected within a mile of a white school. The 1880-1881 report of the superintendent of public instruction shows there were 3,301 white students in Boone County attending 46 schools, 8 of which were log schools. The state appropriation was $5,084. There were 155 "colored" Boone County students attending two schools, both of which were log schools. The state appropriation for the colored schools was $90.[39]

   Roberts rose to the top of the Boone County teaching profession. He was bestowed the title of "Professor Roberts." A professor was one of the fraternity of teachers "making their living that way, and expect to follow it the balance of their days."[40] He was consistently elected to the executive committee of the annual Teacher's Institute. He was selected time and time again to speak at the Teachers Institute. His lectures included such topics as the "Metric System" and the "Purpose of Geographic Study." His speeches included "If my school is not what it should be, who is to blame."[41] Newspaper accounts praised his lectures.

The August 24, 1892 issue of the *Boone County Recorder* listed the top area educators, and it included Roberts:

> T.Z. Roberts is another Boone County bachelor who takes a pleasure in developing the youthful mind, and since 1878 he has spent much of his time in the school-room, surrounded by his neighbors' children. He is well-posted, and defends with vigor, every method he pursues in the school-room.[42]

Besides teaching common school, Roberts taught other schools. He taught "vocal music classes" and at "singing schools." He served as president of the Beech Grove Debate Society.

In 1899 Roberts left the Cason School and traveled to Hebron to teach, boarding with the Alice Crigler family. Roberts' last year of teaching was 1902. He attended the Teacher's Institute in August and, as he had on many occasions, was a speaker at the Institute. His paper was so well received it was published in the newspaper. It gives an idea of Roberts' humor and engaging style:

> The following is the paper read by T. Z. Roberts in the recent Institute, which many of the teachers were anxious to see published.
>
> > I see by the facial expression of the teachers—by the compressed lip and flashing eye—that they are a determined company with an indeterminate power.
> >
> > Here are some of the purposes of the deter-

mined teachers present this morning, if we can judge or conclude by their past words and future deeds: First, then, they are determined to do their best, which is all right, if that best is better than any one else can do.

They have a fixed purpose to teach the primary grades, to read accurately, to spell fluently and to gesticulate melodiously by the following methods: The sentence method, the word method, the combined method and the confounded method—with the alphabet and without it, with script and with print, with pencil and with chalk, with patience and with pain and with any other adjunct or subjunct that may be useful in condensing three days work into ten minutes time.

In ye olden time Teachers thought that the three R's constituted, "first the Blade" in the process of education, but now we think best to teach—to the primary grades especially, civics and physiology before familiarizing them with that which is, you know, really logical, because a definite and masterful knowledge of Civil Government tends to develop civilians and other kinds of villains, and has a broad educational tendency, in teaching mathematics.

The Teachers have a fixed resolution to teach arithmetic in a modest way without egotism or profanity, especially percentage in which they will use the analytic method, the synthetic method, the expansive, the contracted, the fractional the Arithmetical, and the downright upright methods; all of which broaden the view and mystify the mind, and they will teach ration in a ratio-nal manner, of course. That is to be expected.

It is firmly believed by the Teachers that as soon as the primary class has completed the course in Civics, physiology, physiognomy, psychology, biology and anthropology, it should take up the study of spelling and reading, but in this they are willing to defer to the wishes of the patrons.

In writing, the Teachers will allow a letter to slope in any direction except backwards, because the motto of Boone's Teachers is onward and upward.

Now concerning Grammar. I believe it to be the settled purpose of the Teachers of Boone County that even if the idiomatic construction of language depends on Technical Grammar, or if the construction of Technical Grammar depends on idiomatic language, or if the idiotic construction of Grammar depends on technical language, they intend to teach it thoroughly, if they are compelled to learn the latin, the Aryan, Teutonic, or the Russian languages in order to explain it, and they are right, too, for every patron of the school believes that each pupil should be a finished grammarian on leaving school, especially if that pupil be his child. Therefore each Teacher is of unchangeable purpose to drill the pupils in Technical work, Analyzing, Diagramming and Parsing, and to do this thoroughly in the fifteen minutes allowed by the State Program, even if they have classes of 15 or 20 or more. What a noble spirit! What an admirable purpose! never mind the results, the sentiment is there.

Fellow Teachers, I have admired the friendly spirit manifested from each to each in your efforts to assist in making this Institute interesting in your discussions and in those social amenities, which have enlivened and illuminated the week just past, and I am glad that you have decided to carry back to your work that same friendly spirit, that you will have a smile for the patrons, a frown for the Superintendent and a switch for the pupils.[43]

After this last Teacher's Institute, Roberts chose his last school to teach to be at the Locust Grove Schoolhouse. This is where he received his primary education as a boy, where he taught his first school as a teacher and chose it to be his last school before he retired from teaching.

Roberts attended the Morgan Academy as part of his education. It began as the Boone Academy in 1814. For many years it was the highest level of education in Boone County. Photograph provided by Matthew Becher and published in Images of America: Burlington.

Beech Grove Schoolhouse.

Cason Schoolhouse.

*T.Z. Roberts with his class of students in front of the Cason schoolhouse.
The students are as follows: (left to right) back row are T.Z. Roberts ,
Anna Underhill, Ora Ryle, Jim Beemon, Claud Popham, Ella Phipps,
Mae Sandford, Anna Beemon, Argus Popham, Cecil Snelling. Third row are
Hattie White, Edna Cason, Ethel Snelling, Furnish Pope, Unknown,
Unknown, Elmer Goodridge, Unknown Beemon, Cavil Beemon.
Second row are Richard Marshall, Sadie Marshall, Grace Beemon, Unknown,
Unknown, Unknown, Unknown, Unknown, Willie Snelling, Ralph Cason.
Front row are Vernon Pope, Stanley Cason, Ira Ryle.*

CHAPTER SIX

LIFE ON MIDDLE CREEK

T.Z. Roberts lived on Middle Creek his entire life. His parents and the children grew up in a house on the west side of Middle Creek, nearly opposite the place near the creek where Roberts built his first house. Roberts' diary states he was born "in an old frame house on Middle Creek." T.Z. Roberts continued to reside in this house with his parents into his adult years.

Middle Creek was an early center of activity in Boone County. The Middle Creek Road was one of the earliest roads in the county. The area was important in the business sense. Located on Middle Creek was a post office, two water-powered grist mills, a saw mill, a carding mill (for wool), a shingle mill, a grocery store, and a distillery. The area contained 2 churches, one Baptist and one Universalist. Although the Middle Creek Baptist church was Roberts' primary church, he attended the Universalist church on occasion. It was a brick building built on the Jesse Kelly property in 1849. The church building was sold at auction on October 11, 1902 and the land reverted to the Kelly estate.[1]

A review of the *Boone County Recorder* over the years shows several areas around Middle Creek called this area and the Middle Creek Baptist Church as its own. The Neighborhood News section of the *Boone County Recorder* shows the neighborhoods of Reynardsburg, Milling Valley, Commissary, Waterloo and Wayside Gleamings all reporting news of the Middle Creek valley area as their "neighborhood." In the October 7, 1875 *Boone County Recorder* both Milling Valley and Waterloo reported on events at the Middle Creek Baptist Church and Universalist Church. Reynardsburg did not appear in the neighborhood reports until a week later on October 14, 1875. Its first news was on events at the Middle Creek Baptist Church.[2]

On February 8, 1875, at age 24, Roberts purchased 16 acres from his father for $550 to be paid in 16 annual payments. These 16 acres were in the Boone County Cliffs. Roberts immediately began to build a road to the Cliffs and to the "cliff fields" and "cliff cove" as he called them. When his father died the next year on November 23, 1876, the farm was physically divided among the heirs. Roberts and his brother John were appointed administrators of the estate. T.Z. physically assisted in the surveying of the land. Roberts received an additional 19 acres as his part of the inheritance.[3]

By 1880 Roberts was tilling 30 of his acres, and 2 more acres were in hay. His farm was valued at $1,200, and he owned farming implements and machinery valued at $20. He owned 2 horses and 75 poultry. He owned 2 acres of apple orchards with 20 fruit bearing trees. For the year 1879 his farm produced 700 eggs, 200 bushels of Indian corn, 35 bushels of wheat, 2 tons of hay, and 40 bushels of apples.

In 1877 Roberts decided to build a home on his land. It was built on a hill in the cliffs. On September 30, 1877 Roberts wrote:

> I intend to build me a house 16 1/6x 22 1/2 front. I may need a home some time.

His neighbors noticed Roberts was building a house, and the Belleview neighborhood news correspondent reported in the newspaper:

> "Mr. Thomas Z. Roberts has erected a dwelling house on his farm on Middle Creek and is pushing the work rapidly to completion. We understand he is doing the work himself, but when completed, the comforts of it are to be shared with another. Guess it will be a better half.[4]

The house had a rock foundation. Roberts traveled to Aurora, Indiana to get the lumber. The lumber was loaded on skiffs to cross the Ohio River and brought from the river to the cliffs by wagon. It wasn't until March 10, 1880 that Roberts decided the house was finished. Even then he did not move into it, but rented it to Cy Kelly. Roberts continued to maintain his mother's house. For July 23 to 25, 1879 he wrote, "Shingled old house at home." On November 3 to 6, 1879 Roberts wrote, "Helped Aikin build Mothers chimney on creek. Prepared to build my chimney on hill."

It is easy to understand why Roberts built the house and wrote the words "I many need a house some time" as this was the period the 25-year-old Roberts was seriously pursuing the women. It is just as understandable that he stayed and took care of his mother. When his brother John married Frances Craven on November 17, 1877, this meant all of the Roberts children were married except him. This left Roberts to care for his mother, although quite frankly he had plenty of help from his brothers and sisters as they were all a very close family.

When Roberts became engaged to Nora Clore on April 11, 1880, he decided to move into his own home. Her father, Len Clore, helped Roberts crown and plaster his cistern on July 31, 1880. On March 7, 1881 Roberts wrote:

> Hauled part of furniture up to my house—as we are going to move there.

Roberts personally occupied his house "on the hill" from March 7, 1881 until February 8, 1892. Roberts built a new granary on the creek and moved into the granary building on February 8, 1892.

In 1891 Parsons purchased the farm near Roberts. Parsons was a sawmill operator. Roberts and Parsons, if not already good friends at that time, certainly became so over the years. In October of 1891 Roberts helped Parsons dismantle the old Bruce Mill on Middle Creek and turn it into a saw mill. When Mrs. Parsons wanted to open up a grocery store on Middle Creek, it was Roberts who built the storefront addition on to their house. Roberts' diary shows he helped at the sawmill on many occasions and of course, Parsons sawed logs for Roberts.

In June of 1898 Roberts tore down the old Roberts homestead on the creek and brought the lumber across the creek. He used the lumber to build a workshop. As soon as the shop was completed, Roberts began on his last home. Some lumber came from across the river in Aurora, Indiana. Roofing came from Cincinnati, Ohio. Most of the lumber, however, came from the Middle Creek valley.

Roberts' relationship with Parsons undoubtedly had an effect on the quality of wood in the house. Roberts not only chose trees from his land, but his diary show he also went to his neighbors and bought certain of their finer trees. Roberts would personally cut the trees and haul them to Parsons' sawmill. Parsons would allow Roberts a selection from his own finest stock of lumber.

In March of 1900 Roberts dismantled his house on the hill and used it as part of material in his new house. In January and again in May of 1900 Roberts wrote in his diary he made offers to "buy old church," but his offers were not accepted. We do not know for sure what church this was. Possibly, this referred to the Universalist church. We know that the church was, in fact, sold 2 years later. We do know that the large window in the staircase to the second floor contained a large stained glass window.

Most indications are that he moved into the house in January 1901. However, he continued work on the house for some time after that. On February 18, 1901 he wrote "Put in blower-grand improvement." This refers to a shaft that carried air from back of the house to a vent at the base of the fireplace. By adjusting the vent it acted as a blower, and the result was a very hot fire without smoke. He finished the cistern in August of 1901 when he wrote, "fine supply of water." However, Roberts had "tapped" the springs in the cliffs behind his home, and spring water was brought directly to his home. In August of 1903 he "tore down buildings on the hill" and used the lumber to build a 14 x 24 stable.

The house was a work of craftsmanship. Its size is described in Roberts' June 1899 entry in his diary:

> Worked on house all this month, covered it with galvanized steel, house is 28 1/2 x 32 3/4, two story, 8 rooms.

The eight rooms were five bedrooms, a living room, dining room and kitchen. The master bedroom on the first floor contained a two-tier wooden paneled ceiling that Roberts called his suspended ceiling. Roberts' bedroom was on the second floor where he built a "swinging bed." It was suspended from the ceiling so he could rock himself to sleep. The dining room and kitchen could be divided by sliding partitions. Above the fireplace Roberts carved the letters GOD in the mantel. Over the mantel surrounding the stained glass window Roberts carved "TZ Roberts Builder 1900."

Roberts did not indicate why he built such a large and beautiful home. Josephine Cason wrote that Roberts was "not satisfied" with his house on the hill and that he decided he would build him a nice home so his brothers and sisters might "come home too, once in a while."[5] The cliffs on his farm had been the site of the family reunion for many years, and after this house was built family members came to live with him over the years.

In the obituary of the senior Thomas Roberts, he was described as a master of the science of carpentry. His son certainly was interested in carpentry, and Roberts developed into a master craftsman whose services were also sought after over the years. A review of Roberts' diary and other papers reveal Roberts built just about everything. Examples include ice skates (Roberts was a renowned ice skater)[6]; a square fiddle; a violin; croquet balls; money box; wind engine; shingle making machine; jigsaw, forge; flute; wheel spokes; bee hives for himself and for sale; pulley blocks; school benches; angle meter; tables; double shovel plow; harrow plow; workbench; vise; washing machine; wheelbarrow; desk; bobsled; wagon; horse drawn sleds; handles for axes, chisel, etc.[7]

He built numerous houses during his life. In November 1882 he was paid $1.50 a day to work on Tom Rouse's house. He built a house for Georgia Clore in 1907 for $68 which took about 1 1/2 months to complete. In the summer of 1924, at age 74, he was building a house for Linny Love.

Roberts also built many barns, remodeled kitchens, built a "hennery," granaries, and a smokehouse, and constructed fences, storehouses and other work. By today's standards his work was cheap. For example, in the fall of 1890 he was paid $27.80 for building a barn for Henry Clore. In January of 1891 he was paid $5 for building a smokehouse for Dock Clore. In July of 1892 he was paid $3.75 for building fence for A. Cason. Of course, materials were cheaper. In his diary Roberts mentions he bought a whole keg of 10- inch nails on September 19, 1894 for $2.

One of his other monuments that still stands is the Belleview Baptist Church. In 1903 he worked on the building of the church. His diary notes that in May of 1903 he "searched for rock for the new church building," and he later wrote, "get up rock for ch." He worked steadily on the church under the direction of architect H. Griffith. The words, "Jesus Saves," which were carved in the arched opening in the window behind the pulpit, were the handiwork of Roberts.

Josephine Cason wrote that her uncle T.Z. Roberts "was never idle very much in his younger life."[8] Roberts was an active farmer and miller, which skills he also learned from his father. He wrote that he plowed corn at 11 years of age. When he commenced his diary it is apparent that he had been farming and milling for his father. He would work for other people such as when he, at age 21 in November 1872, "Worked for Bob Rice for 85¢ per day snapping corn." Shortly thereafter his brother John, his closest brother in age, yet eight years older than T.Z., agreed to rent his land to Roberts to farm in return for one-third of the yield. Roberts grew tobacco, wheat, corn, and grapes. His diary notes John and he went to Aurora, Indiana and Cincinnati, Ohio to sell their grapes. The next year, upon his return from the Morgan

Academy, Roberts "hired" himself to his father for the summer for $150. He worked the farm and in the mill. Some nights he would spend the entire night working in the mill, something he would do throughout his milling career.

That same summer, on August 2, 1874, Roberts joined the Patrons of Husbandry. This organization was a farmers' protective society multiplying over the country in an effort to combat the depressive trend of farm products created by the Panic of 1873. The Kentucky Chapters resolved themselves into local political clubs that tried to obtain special concessions from the Kentucky General Assembly. One of its main purposes was to exert a major influence upon the elections of candidates.[9] Four months later, on December 4, 1874, Roberts was elected as secretary of the Grange. He quickly gained the respect of his fellow citizens and farmers, as this published account of a Grange meeting illustrates:

> Wm. Conner was chosen to install the officers for the ensuing year, in the presence of a large concourse of spectators. He arose and stated that he felt himself inadequate to the duty devolving upon him, but made a short but appropriate speech, in which he stated the Grange represented a farm, master, overseer, & c., that persons present might understand and appreciate the installation ceremonies, which were very imposing, only enlivened by the stirring music of the well appointed and efficient band. After his, speeches were called for—first the name of Zane!Zane!
>
> And Zane arose, and in a stentorian voice exclaimed: "An architect cannot build a structure without a foundation, he that hath nothing to say, let him say nothing." And Zane was heard no more.[10]

The Grangers were certainly a social group as well. They annually held a Harvest Feast. Held each August, all the local chapters of the Boone County Grange would attend. The Feast would open with a parade headed by a brass band. All the Grangers would be in the procession. Local chapters in Boone County would include East Bend, Belleview, Mt. Pleasant, Petersburg, Pomona, Point Pleasant, Speedwell and Mt. Zion. The program would continue with guest speakers, dinner, local speakers and then dancing. If it got too dark, the dancing would be moved to the Morgan Academy.[11]

Roberts would attend the Harvest Feast on a regular basis. He was a well-known speaker and was chosen to speak at these events. A newspaper account of the 1878 Harvest Feast reported:

> Mr. T.Z. Roberts was the next orator. He chose to discuss "Shall Young Folks Join the Grange?"His remarks were brief but strongly support the affirmative of the proposition.[12]

Six months after Roberts joined the Grange his father sold him the 16 acres of land to farm. A little over a year later the senior Roberts died, leaving T.Z. as the person left at home to care for Mrs. Roberts.

When the senior Roberts died he had already sold 38 1/2 acres of his farm to his neighbor John Cox on March 19, 1870. The remainder was divided as follows:

Lot 1	Belle Cason	21 acres
Lot 2	Theodore Roberts	22 acres
Lot 3	Annie French	28 acres
Lot 4	Mary Craven	24 1/2 acres
Lot 5	John O. Roberts	19 acres
Lot 6	Thomas Z. Roberts	19 acres
Lot 7	Ella J. Beasley	22 acres
DOWER INTEREST		
	Roxanne Roberts	50 acres

Roberts immediately started the process of purchasing the interest of his siblings to reunite the farm back to its original 221-

plus acres. This was not easy for Roberts to do with his meager income at age 25. He still owed money on the original 16 acres he had purchased from his father, and now he owed it to his sisters and brothers.

In the old justice of the peace book he started his accounts as follows:

Accounts with Heirs 1879

Theodore DV.

to cash	3.00
to acct & notes	5.10
to Mill acct.	4.74
to 5 bu. wheat	7.00
to 25 lbs. flour	.75
to share certificates	10.00
	30.59

John DV.

to cash	3.00
to acct of Beeman	3.20
to note	.10
to 2 Bu. Meal	1.20
to cash	10.00
to cert. of stock	10.00

Annie DV.

| to cash | 10.00 |
| to note & inst. | 33.60 |

Mary DV.

to cash	3.00
to notes & inst.	14.50
to notes bought	2.00
to bal. on corn	2.15
to 3 bu. camper cox	1.20

Belle DV.

to cash	3.00
to cash	5.00
to cert. of stock	10.00

Ella DV.

to cash	3.00
to acct.	5.30
to note on Holand	.75
to 5 Bu. corn	3.00
to share of certificate	10.00

Over his lifetime Roberts attempted to reunify the family farm. When he conveyed the farm to his nephew Ralph Zane Cason on March 16, 1917, the farm consisted of 154 acres, which he acquired as follows:

1) 16 acres – the original 16 acres he purchased from his father for $600.

2) 19 acres – Lot 6 he received as his share of inheritance

3) 1 acre 30 poles – Purchased from the trustee of the Middle Creek Baptist Church for

$35.62 (December 3, 1877)

4)   21 acres – Purchased Lot 1 from sister
        Belle Cason on April 28, 1882 for $315.

5)   50 acres 1 Rod 30 poles – Purchased
        mother's dower interest from his brothers
        and sisters for $600. on June 29, 1886

6)   28 1/2 acres – Purchased Lot 4 and four
        acres of Lot 3 from sister Mary Craven
        for $600.

7)   19 acres – This was Lot 5 of the farm
        division received by John Roberts. He sold
        it to W. H. Beasley on July 16, 1877 for
        $600 and Beasley in turn sold it to
        John Acra. It was sold on April 12, 1889 to
        Roberts for $500.

8)   64 1/ 2 perches – Purchased from Reuben
        and Permilia Acra on March 30, 1888
        for $7.75

Shortly after conveying the farm to nephew Ralph, Roberts purchased 22 more acres on Middle Creek from Laura Belle Parsons (formerly Marshall) on January 2, 1919. Roberts then conveyed this property to his nephew Ralph Cason.

Roberts grew many commodities on his farm including tobacco, corn, wheat, grapes, and potatoes. He grafted and planted apple trees over the years on his farm. As late as the time of his death he maintained two separate orchards. He noted in March of 1906 he grafted 800 apple trees. The previous year, on November 23, 1905 he wrote "set valley greening apple trees on old church lot." Roberts also maintained beehives. He apparently kept a lookout for bees during swarming season. You can sense the excitement in his diary when he found swarming bees, which he would go out and catch. He made his own beehives and sold beehives that he had made.

Most of his income from farming came from the products of tobacco, corn and wheat. The tobacco would be sold at various tobacco warehouses. Corn and wheat would be ground at his mill and sold at local stores or taken to Indiana for sale. It is interesting to see the prices he received over the years for his tobacco and how he might go to a place to sell his tobacco only to change his mind because the price was too low. He would take his tobacco home to resell another day. The following are some examples from his diary:

July 22, 1875	sold tobacco at Globe House
April 9, 1877	took tobacco to Rabbit Hash
July 23, 1877	Haul tobacco to Carlton
June 26, 1880	Walked 6 miles after tobacco plants
May 30, 1882	Haul tobacco (1286 lbs.)
June 1, 1882	Haul trash (430 lbs.) received for tobacco $178.35
October 14, 1882	Have about 1400 sticks of tobacco
June 19, 1885	Finish hauling old tobacco 1823 lbs. brought me $75.00
February 8, 1886	went to Boone Rogers to sell tobacco – no sale
February 9, 1886	went to F Wingales to sell tobacco – no sale
February 15, 1886	Went again to Boone Rogers to sell tobacco – no sell
February 16, 1886	Tobacco weighed 3,700 lbs.
May 3, 1887	sold tobacco at 4 1/2¢, 2¢, and 1¢ per lbs.
April 8, 1890	Reach Louisville
April 9, 1890	Sell tobacco at Enterprise House at 9.90, 3.50, 3.05
March 8, 1892	Start to Louisville with tobacco
March 9, 1892	on the breaks. reject.
March 10, 1892	Return home

| April 2, 1892 | Went to Burlington to get check cashed. Sold 7 HHd. Tobacco (8,445 lbs) for $529 Net. |

As mentioned above, Roberts also raised corn and wheat and he would either sell it by the bushel or grind and sell the meal:

August 27, 1883	sell wheat at Lawrenceburg
October 5, 1884	went to Rising Sun to sell wheat – did not sell— too low
April 2, 1887	sold corn 456.88
June 19, 1889	Haul corn 163 bu $57.15
January 4, 1895	sell 100 lbs. corn $45

One of the most interesting entries in Roberts' diary is in March of 1902, when he writes, "Carlos and I sold our tobacco 4915 lbs for $344.16." On March 18, 1902 Roberts writes, "go to Cincinnati to buy telescope." On March 20, 1902 he writes "Rented farm to Ben Cason (his brother-in-law) for $200 per year. He moved down." After Roberts bought the telescope, there is not one mention in his diary about selling farm products or planting corn or wheat for sale.

The mills on Middle Creek had long been a part of Boone County history. It is likely that the Garnett Mill was around before Boone County was established. It was the first water grist mill officially permitted by the county court to dam a creek as reported in Order Book A on July 9, 1804. The only lands injured by the dam were those of Humphrey Marshall. Thereafter, Humphrey Marshall was permitted by order of the county court dated April 2, 1810 in Order Book A to establish a water grist and saw mill on Middle Creek with a dam 10 feet in height. As a result, the road from the courthouse to Tolberts ferry had to be closed.

For many years the milling business was a big part of Roberts' life. His father, when he first moved to Middle Creek, operated the "Garnett Mill" with John Riddell. Roberts grew up working in the mill. Many times he stayed in the mill and worked all night, undoubtedly because the creek was running hard at that time to push the wheel and grindstone. Roberts took a renewed interest in the mill in 1879 after finishing up his father's estate. He wrote as follows:

April 28 to 30, 1879	Took charge of mill and refitted it
May 1 to 3, 1879	Work on Mill
May 5 to 7, 1879	Mill Business took meal to L. Aylor (a local store on Garnett Mill— Middle Creek Road)
May 8, 1879	Took meal to Belleview

As part of the census in 1880 the U.S. Government took an inventory of grist mills in the country. This census provides an insight into the mills on Middle Creek.

The Roberts mill was an overshot water mill. The height of the fall was 41 feet. The breadth was 39 feet. It produced 64 horsepower and 3 revolutions per minute. It had 2 runs of stone and had a capacity of 75 bushels per day. It operated full time 10 months per year and was idle 2 months per year. Some of the time was devoted to custom grinding. For the year 1879 the mill produced 1,050 barrels of wheat flour, 200 pounds of buckwheat flour, 323,815 pounds of corn meal and 12,700 pounds of feed. The products were valued at $3,700.

A short distance down Middle Creek, James Bruce was operating the other grist mill. It was also an overshot water mill, although a bit smaller than the Roberts mill. Its height of fall was 36 feet, and it had a breadth of 25 feet. It did 3 revolutions per minute with a horsepower of 42. In 1879 the Bruce mill produced 107,700 pounds of corn meal and 18,000 pounds of feed. Bruce milled 10,800 bushels of wheat. The total value of the finished products was $2,400.

For several years Roberts continued the mill business. However, over time he did less and less milling until he ceased altogether. In 1906 he decided to reopen the mill using a gasoline powered engine. He bought the engine in Cincinnati for $213 in May 1906.[13] He built a 12 x 24 mill building and milled that summer and fall. He decided "the expense was too great to be profitable so I shipped the engine back to Cincinnati, Ohio and sold it so as to lose about $200."[14]

The local community was sad to see Roberts quit the milling business as this newspaper article reveals:

> T. Z. Roberts sold his gasoline engine to the party of whom he purchased it. Middle Creek is now without a mill.[15]

The gasoline engine was again in the newspaper on May 8, 1907:

> The gasoline engine that T. Z. Roberts sold and shipped to a party in Cincinnati was badly broken when loading it on the transfer wagon. The breakage will cost $50 to repair.[16]

Roberts' life gives us a good history of the development of Boone County from the post Civil War days until World War I. At the beginning of this period, travel was usually by foot or horseback. Roberts was a great walker. He wore high leather boots with straps. When walking he would pull his trousers up high atop his boots, but in the schoolroom he would pull the trousers over his boots.[17] When he taught at Locust Grove he walked to school, a distance of approximately 3 miles. It wasn't until the 1870s that roads became developed enough in Boone County to make travel by horse and buggy more common.

When the Roberts family took up residence on Middle Creek in the last part of the 1840s the road system was in its infancy in Boone County. The following were the privately maintained turnpikes in Boone County in 1850:

Union and Florence	5.5 miles
Union and Beaverlick	5.0 miles
White Haven and Richwood	2.5 miles
Burlington and Florence	6.0 miles
Beaverlick and Richwood	5.0 miles
Cincinnati and Lexington	11.0 miles[18]

Although by the 1870s roads were being developed, travel was still a problem.

The editor of the *Boone County Recorder* wrote on February 17, 1876 that "Loud is the complaint of bad roads" and "Dirt roads still have bottoms, but a horse goes a long way down to find it."[19] Even the turnpikes had their problems. On September 23, 1875 the *Boone County Recorder* reported in its maiden issue, "The Petersburg and Burlington Turnpike has been in sad repair for some time past, but preparation is now being made to give a portion of the road a new coat of stone."[20] In the Middle Creek area the roads were even worse. On January 27, 1876 the Middle Creek area reported, "We are having bad roads to travel now, and if the rains continue, expect still worse."[21] Less than two months later the newspaper reported, "The roads near here are almost impassable, the mud being as deep as, or deeper than, it has been this winter."[22] On a trip to go to Rising Sun, H. P. Parson and William Clore reported that parts of the roads had no bottom.[23]

The conditions of bridges may have not been much better. This following article about the nearby Woolper area reports:

> Last Saturday the bridge across Woolper Creek, on the road leading from Bellevue[now Belleview] to Petersburg, gave way and fell while one Israel Smith, with a four horse team and a wagon loaded with corn were crossing it. The distance of the fall was about twenty feet and the back water into which the man, team and bridge were plunged was about five feet

deep. In a few moments assistance arrived, and after struggling with the frightened horses and mules near two hours in chilly water and mud, and the fragments of the bridge, the men succeeded in extricating the team, while some think will never be of any value in consequence of the injuries resulting from the disaster. One of the horses was so excited as to be perfectly frantic and one or two men narrowly escaped being killed by it some time after it was taken from the wreck. Mr. Smith, the driver of the team, miraculously escaped with slight injuries. This was a new bridge, recently erected at considerable expense to some of the immediate neighborhood, to say nothing about the $500 the county gave toward the erection.[24]

A turnpike between Belleview and Burlington, which would pass through the Middle Creek Valley and through the Dinsmore farm (now Ky. 18), was chartered on February 3, 1851. Construction didn't begin until 1877.[25] Momentum for support of construction of the road developed in 1876. An October 5, 1876 article reported:

"That a turnpike leading from Burlington to Bellevue[now Belleview] will mutually increase the value of the farms by and through which it will run can not be denied . . .The investment will certainly in a short time yield a handsome dividend, because it will soon become one of the principal thoroughfares in the county. Much of the travel to the city that is now done by way of the river prefer the road, because of its being a shorter and cheaper route to the city . . ."[26]

Two weeks later a letter to the editor of the *Boone County Recorder* supporting the road stated;

> We are pleased to see so much spirit and zeal developing in favor of prosecuting to completion, the proposed turnpike leading from Burlington to Bellevue[now Belleview]. Some of the best and most thorough business men along the route have taken the matter in hand and are pushing the scheme forward with a determination which augurs for success . . . For a number of years the people of the county between Bellevue[now Belleview] and Burlington have been making spasmodic efforts to procure a convenient and good outlet but have never been able to fix upon any but the present proposed route, and in fact, no other feasible plan can be adopted, and of this all are now thoroughly convinced . . .The road will furnish the only necessary link to make a continuous pike from the Ohio River, at Bellevue[now Belleview] to the City of Covington, and with it completed, the trip may be made from Bellevue[now Belleview] to Cincinnati in four hours in a horse and buggy. From Rising Sun to Cincinnati the trip may be made in five hours. The distance from Bellevue[now Belleview] to Cincinnati by water is about forty miles. The distance by way of the completed road will be about twenty-three miles, making a difference of seventeen miles.[27]

By November 30, 1876 the road was reported to have been engineered.[28] On December 7, 1876 notice to contractors were let for "grading, McAdamizing, bridging, building culverts and completing the road."[29]

The road was not built without problems. At one point in time it appeared the contractors were leaving the job, causing a near-violent confrontation between the subscribers to the project and the contractor, Wake & Burgis.[30] A tollgate was erected in October 1877 even before the road was completely finished.[31]

Even though an improved toll road was built between Burlington and Belleview and passed right by Middle Creek, the next half-century showed no improvement for the inhabitants of Middle Creek for travel to their homes. A newspaper article in 1902 reported:

> "Since the announcement that Santa Claus will make his annual rounds this year in an automobile, the people on Middle Creek are afraid he will not visit them on account of the bad conditions of the roads. Don't be alarmed. Arrangements have been made by which if the present stage of water exists at Christmas, he will travel from Belleview to the Parsons mill road, where he will leave his auto and go up Middle Creek in a dory; but if the stage of water is not sufficient, he will go up on a mud sled, or, as is called by some people, a mud boat.[32]

Ten years later in 1913 showed no improvement:

> Auto Truck Stalled on Middle Creek Boulevard
> Theo. Heck & Co.'s furniture truck went down to Carl Cason's Tuesday with a load of furniture, and just before reaching the house the truck stuck in the mud, the hind axle going down to the ground. Middle Creek roads were not constructed with a view to the operation of auto thereon.[33]

The same year in 1913, the road conditions prompted the following article in the Middle Creek section of the newspaper:

> Don't forget to drag the mud roads. If you will begin now and keep the good work up all the winter you

will come through the winter without being stuck in the mud. Take the section of mud road adjoining your farm and see if you can not keep it in better condition than your neighbor keeps the section adjoining his farm.[34]

People in Middle Creek were still getting their mail delivered by horseback in 1913.[35]

Roberts walked or traveled by horse. He kept one or more horses. His diary identifies three of them, namely Beg, Kate and Ray. His favorite was Kate, which he bought when Roberts was 21 years of age on October 16, 1872 for $72 from C. Sedam. Kate was about 12 years old at that time. She was his main means of travel for many years. He bred her and sold her colts. She died on October 29, 1892 at the age of 32 years. He also owned a buggy and wagon that he used for travel. When he built his last beautiful house in 1900, he built a buggy shed next to it to store the buggy. Many years later his nephew Ralph Cason would use the buggy shed to store his automobile.

When Roberts needed supplies, or if he was selling his farm's products, he had several options. He would go to the R.L. Aylor store at the corner of Waterloo and East Bend Road. Of course, nearby was his favorite cousin, Zillah E. Green, as well as H.P. Marshall (father of Maggie Marshall) and Leonard Clore (father of Nora Clore). He also visited Belleview quite frequently for supplies. The 1883 Atlas lists the following "Bellevue Business References." The 1883 Atlas still referred to "Belleview" as "Bellevue."

> G.B. MCMULLEN, CONTRACTOR AND BUILDER, DEALER IN MIXED AND LIQUID PAINTS, LEADS, OILS, BRUSHES, VARNISHES & C. HOUSE AND SIGN PAINTING OF EVERY DESCRIPTIONS. ALSO DEALER IN LEAF TOBACCO AND WHARFMASTER. GRANT P.O.

A. CORBIN, DEALER IN DRY GOODS, GRO-
CERIES, HATS, CAPS, BOOTS, SHOES,
QUEENSWARE, TINWARE, HARDWARE,
AND EVERYTHING USUALLY KEPT IN
FIRST CLASS COUNTY STORE. ALSO A
FULL STOCK OF LUMBERS, SHINGLES,
SALT AND COAL. THE PUBLIC WILL DO
WELL TO CALL ON ME BEFORE PURCHAS-
ING ELSEWHERE.
H.C. BOTTS, DEALER IN LEAF TOBACCO.
WILL PAY THE HIGHEST MARKET PRICE
FOR FIRST-CLASS TOBACCO.
W.W. GRANT, BLACKSMITHING AND
WAGON-MAKING IN ALL ITS BRANCHES
DONE WITH NEATNESS, ACCURACY AND
DISPATCH. MACHINERY PROMPTLY
REPAIRED. HORSE-SHOEING SPECIALTY.[36]

Roberts frequently went to Rising Sun and Aurora. His sister Annie lived in Rising Sun, and he would visit her often. He
traveled to Indiana by going to McVille and catching the ferry. The
ferry was operated by horses. An 1876 newspaper article shows the
cost of crossing the ferry at Belleview was 60¢ each way and from
Rabbit Hash was 75¢ each way.[37] Roberts noted in his diary that
many times he would go to the ferry and find himself unable to
cross because the water was too dangerous, too low, or simply the
horses weren't available. The Ohio River was very different then as
compared to present times. The river water was crystal clear, and
the beaches in Dayton and Bellevue (in Campbell County) were a
national attraction. The river normally averaged about 7 feet deep,
and during dry periods people could walk across the river. The
river in 1881, because of a drought, was only 1.9 feet at Covington
on September 17. Where the Ohio River looped around Boone
County the river at times during the dry season would be only a
foot deep. During the flood of 1884, it reached a peak of 71.1 feet.
In 1924 a lock and dam, No. 38, were built at McVille. They were

replaced in 1962 by the Markland Dam. The average depth of the pool of the Ohio River after the dam is 26 feet.[38]

Rising Sun and Aurora apparently offered things Roberts couldn't get locally. For example:

December 6, 1872	Belle, Ella and I got to Aurora – get some fine pictures taken
June 6, 1873	Ma very sick – went to Rising Sun after physician
September 13, 1878	went to Rising Sun for boots
August 21, 1880	go to Rising Sun to get teeth pulled
October 28, 1891	buy a suit of clothes at Rising Sun for $16.00
April 29, 1892	go to Rising Sun for grindstone
September 29, 1894	buy a keg of 10d nails for $2 at R.S.

Roberts also traveled to Cincinnati, Ohio on occasions to purchase items. Among the trips to Cincinnati his diary notes that on June 21, 1875 he went to Clark's store to get a Bible, and he bought an organ on December 7, 1882. Of course, his famous telescope was bought in Cincinnati.

An early photograph of the Roberts house.

This photograph is of a reunion taken during the construction of the house and before the building was built in which the solar clock was constructed.

Photographs were taken and commonly placed on postcards. This postcard is of T.Z. Roberts and family in front of his home. Roberts is seated in the middle. The postcard was sent from his sister Belle to her son Carlos on October 19, 1907.

Stairway: "T Z Roberts Builder 1900."

Master bedroom containing suspended ceiling.

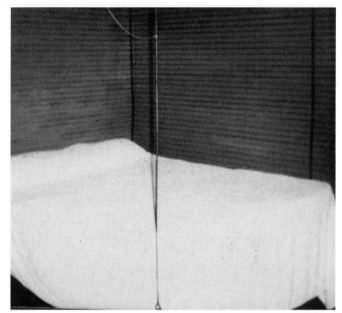

Roberts' swinging bed.

Fireplace in Roberts' living room.
Notice blower and hand-carving of G O D on mantle.

Grindstone from Roberts' mill.

Outlet to spring from the Middle Creek Cliffs that Roberts tapped to bring fresh water to his home. Notice the water still flowed in 1975.

Roberts' tobacco field was on one side of Middle Creek, and his barn was on the other side at a distance of approximately 600 feet. He constructed a pulley system to carry the tobacco. He would place the tobacco on the pulley system near the tobacco field, and its own weight would carry the tobacco from the field to the barn.

This photograph shows the sorghum mill on the Roberts farm. Irene Cason is on the horse, and left to right are Luella Cason, Grandpa Stephens, Bill Koons and Ralph Cason.

This photograph is taken in front of the cave at Middle Creek Cliffs. Thomas Z. Roberts is at the far right. Also pictured are Carl Cason, Leona Cason, Mae Sandford, Roxanna Cason, Wendell Phipps, Ella Phipps and Tommy Cason.

This photograph shows a better picture of the cave at Middle Creek Cliffs, which were part of Roberts' farm. The photograph was taken on May 6, 1934.

This old photograph was found in the Roberts/Cason family archives.

*Hog slaughtering on Roberts/Cason Middle Creek farm.
The Boone County Cliffs are on the right.*

Old postcard of downtown Burlington. Notice the dirt roads.

Old Middle Creek Road upon leaving the Old Middle Creek Baptist Church and Cemetery traveled the highest ridge in Middle Creek and went to Kelly Road and East Bend Road. Roberts would have used this road to get to Locust Grove School House, Beech Grove School House, the Universalist Church, Nora Clore's home, Maggie Marshall's home, and Aylor's store. This was called the Garnett Mill-Big Bone Lick Road.

The above is from the 1883 Atlas of Boone County.
The author has added the following: 1) Middle Creek Baptist Church 2)
Locust Grove School House 3) Beech Grove School House
4) Roberts' last home, where the solar clock stood for 64 years.

CHAPTER SEVEN

THE DINSMORE MIDDLE CREEK PLANTATION

While Thomas Zane Roberts Sr. and Roxanne Odell Roberts were staking their claim in Boone County a similar situation was happening right down the road with the Dinsmore family. While the Roberts family came from New Jersey, James Dinsmore and Silas Dinsmoor were from New Hampshire. Silas was the uncle of James. Both were educated at Dartmouth College. Silas was born in 1766. James was born in 1790. James was the second-oldest of eight brothers and sisters. James' father died in 1814, and a special relationship developed between James and his Uncle Silas. James' father had changed the spelling of the family name from "Dinsmoor" to "Dinsmore" while brother Silas kept the old way of spelling the family name.

James Dinsmore married Martha Macomb. She was the daughter of Alexander Macomb, Sr. Their New York City home was used as the executive mansion by George Washington during his first term as president of the United States.

Silas lived in Cincinnati around 1830. In 1831 Silas purchased a farm in Belleview, Boone County, Kentucky. Silas was a land surveyor for the federal government and had difficulty getting paid, and for some time he was dependent upon James for money. James helped Silas purchase the Boone County farm.

Meanwhile, James moved to Natchez, Mississippi around 1815 and studied law in the office of Judge Turner. While in Mississippi James tutored William Minor's nephews. Around 1820 Minor and James became partners in cotton and sugar planting. They purchased a sugar and cotton plantation in Louisiana. James managed the plantation while Minor stayed in Natchez,

Mississippi.[1]

In 1831 James wrote to Uncle Silas and indicated he would be interested in purchasing property on the Ohio River. He also wrote that he would be interested in cultivating grapes. In 1834 James wrote to Silas and told him that he obtained grapes from South Carolina but the land in Louisiana was not conducive to vineyards and wanted to know if the soil there was appropriate. He indicated that he was tired of sugar planting; "It is hard work and little profit."[2]

Letters followed over the next several years indicating his interest in purchasing land in Kentucky. In 1838 James came to Boone County and looked at land to purchase. By October 1838 a deal was made to purchase the Clore farm.[3] Over the next several years James developed the property into a working farm in absentia through use of tenants and managers. Trees were girdled and land turned into pasture. Fruit trees and grape vines were grown.

While still in Louisiana, James designed his home to be built in Middle Creek. His brother John and James' cousin Thomas Dinsmore undertook the construction of the home. The house was completed in 1842. By the summer of 1842 James was living on his Middle Creek farm with his wife, Martha, and their three daughters, Isabella (DOB 1830), Julia (DOB 1833), and Susan (DOB 1835).

Although the Dinsmore family lived in the Middle Creek valley since 1842 and the Roberts family since 1846, there is little recorded information on their interaction. A grinding stone from the Roberts mill still stands at the back door of the Dinsmore house and was used as a platform for children to mount their horse.[4] T.Z. Roberts mentioned in his diary attending a sing at the Dinsmores.[5] Julia Dinsmore had a similar interest in literature as Roberts. She had her poems published by *Doubleday* and in the *New Orleans Times Democrat*. Brother Theodore Roberts sold 10 acres of his land on Middle Creek for a one half interest in one year's tobacco crop on the Dinsmore farm.[6] Julia Dinsmore attended Sunday School and preaching services at the Middle

Creek Church and later Belleview Baptist. Two of the Dinsmore's slaves were baptized into the Middle Creek Church and were regular members. Julia was good personal friends with Middle Creek Church's pastor, Robert E. Kirtley.[7] Middle Creek road connected with the Burlington Belleview Road near the Dinsmore plantation, and the Roberts family members would have passed the Dinsmore plantation on a regular basis.

The Dinsmores' interest in crops was a bit different than most other farmers on Middle Creek. They did raise tobacco, wheat and corn on their 800-acre farm. They also established orchards. James had a keen interest in fruit trees. He raised apple, peach, pear, cherry and plum trees, investing in several varieties of each fruit. He kept notes on how each did and made cider from the ripened fruit. He had beehives. James also attempted a few more unusual crops. Two years before the Dinsmores moved into their Middle Creek house, James sent Osage orange tree seeds to Silas to be planted on his farm. In a letter from James to Silas he wrote:

> It is valuable for a hedge, is a substitute for fustic as a dye and binder is one of the strongest and most elastic woods known in the country. Please have part of the seed sown on my creek bottoms and engage one of my tenants to attend to it carefully for me.[8]

James Dinsmore's experience with the Osage orange tree proved to be a satisfying experience. He wrote a letter to the Genesee Farmer, a New York publication, and the letter was reprinted in the *Covington Journal* on October 26, 1849:

> Agricultural, & c.
> From the Genesee Farmer.
> Thorn Hedges-The Osage Orange

> Messers Editors: -In the June number of your valuable paper you invite correspondents, who have had experience in growing hedges to communicate the result: I have been making experiments for several

years, principally with the Osage Orange, with the most flattering success. Among the plants I have seen tried for hedgeing [sic] are the Cherokee Rose, the Osage Orange, the Honey Locust, the Hawthorn and the Buckthorn. The former in the States south of Tennessee, makes an excellent and highly ornamental hedge. I have tried it here, but it is too tender for this latitude. In Louisiana it forms a hedge which is impassable to the wildest animals, but the farmers complain that it affords a harbor for multitudes of rats, snakes and wasps. The objection to the Honey Locust is that it is of too large a growth and difficult to be kept down. The Hawthorn is devoured by insects, and soon perishes.

The Osage Orange, I consider the beau ideal of hedge plants. It is a native of Louisiana, and is stated to be hardy at Boston, and will undoubtedly succeed from the Gulf of Mexico to the Lakes. In my opinion it would be difficult to estimate the value of this plant to the United States too highly. Englishmen have confessed to me, that they have no plant in Europe to be compared to this, for hedgeing [sic] purposes. A piece of the root 3 or 4 inches long planted [in sandy soil] with the top a little below the surface, will produce a plant in one season, from 2 to 6 feet high.

There is some difficulty in growing plants from the dry seeds, without preparation. If planted dry, not one in twenty will grow. When taken fresh from the half decayed ball or fruit they will grow as readily as peas. If dry, soak them a few hours in milk—warm water; pour off the water and stir in fresh ashes, and let them remain moist three or four days. –Then sow in drills an inch deep in rich and well prepared ground, and when the plants appear keep them clear from weeds. When you wish to plant in hedge, cut off the top two inches above the ground, take up the plants, cut off the principal roots, leaving the main tap root 8 inches long. Plant in two rows from 6 to 12 inches apart, and keep the ground clean. The spring following, cut down the plants to 6 inches. The second year leave them a foot high and leave a portion of the largest shoots to be interlocked with each other. The third year leave them two feet, and the fourth year 4 feet high. After this you may regulate the height to suit your fancy. The hedge will then present a dense mass of shoots covered with thorns, almost as sharp as needles, and averaging a thorn for every inch in length of the branches.

I have not observed that any insect preys on this plant, but Dr. White, of Ohio, informed me that the largest cocoons he had ever seen were from silk worms fed on its leaves. I have supposed, that its exemption from injury by insects was owing to the acrid milky juice, which the leaves exude. I have a hedge around my vineyard, a part of which is of four years growth. Not a plant had died out, and it presents an impenetrable mass of branches, thorns and glossy leaves, which is truly beautiful. It will afford a most efficient protection to a fruit garden or vineyard, and I cannot conceive a more embarrassing [sic] situation for a vagabond, than attempting to pass through such a hedge with a fierce dog at his heels.

It is probable that the tops of the plants would be killed by the frost in New York the first winter, but that would do no permanent injury. The wood of the Osage Orange is exceedingly strong, elastic and durable, and is used by the Indians of the west for bows, whence the French name of Bois d'Arc, by which it is known on the Red River.

J. Dinsmore
Boone County, Ky., July, 1849[9]

The Osage orange tree did establish itself throughout the Middle Creek valley and is still abundantly providing fruit for the wildlife.

The Dinsmore plantation also raised sheep for their wool. William Conrad in his *A Journey into the Past* maintains that at one time Middle Creek had a carding mill, which mill would comb and clean wool of burrs and knots making it more suitable for spinning into yarn.[10] He also raised goats. When James died in 1872 he had over 40 goats and over 30 sheep.

For a period of time a ham and sausage business was run on the Dinsmore plantation by James' granddaughter, Patty Selmes, and her business partner, Sally Wooly, in the late 1890s into the 1900s. Hog farming had long been a staple product of the farms in the Middle Creek area. The early *Boone County Recorder* contain many stories of hog raising and slaughtering on the "Reynardsburg" and "Waterloo" neighborhood farms.[11] Nora Clore's father, Leonard Clore, who farmed over 10,000 acres in 1850, raised many hogs along with his cattle and sheep.[12]

Dinsmore also grew willows on his farm. He did not use the wild willows but planted a variety used in basket weaving called the Osiers. He established a basket factory on Middle Creek. He employed between 6 and 12 basket makers. In 1870 seven of the county's 14 basket makers worked in Belleview for Dinsmore. He shipped out as many as 30,000 pounds of surplus willow switches each time a steamboat stopped at the Belleview port. Willow switches brought about $50 per ton in the 1860s.[13] It appears April and May were the ideal willow stripping periods. In the *Boone County Recorder* for April 17, 1913 it stated, "Willow stripping time will soon be here."[14] A May issue for the same newspaper stated, "The willow growers are most through stripping and the crop is all it could be desired."[15]

Martha Dinsmore died on August 17, 1859. James Dinsmore died on December 21, 1872. The youngest daughter Susan, drowned in an accident in July 1851 at age 15. The oldest daughter, Isabella, married on August 10, 1859 in the Dinsmore home. She had two daughters, but Isabella died six months after the birth of her second daughter in 1866. This left Julia to inherit the farm. She never married. She maintained the farm until her death in 1926. She was instrumental in raising her sister Isabella's two daughters on the Dinsmore plantation. Isabella's oldest daughter, Martha, and her husband became lifelong personal friends of Teddy Roosevelt. Martha's daughter Isabella was born at the Dinsmore house. She was the bridesmaid at the wedding of Eleanor and Franklin Delano Roosevelt.

The Dinsmore story is interesting, and much can be told. The most interesting fact is the Dinsmore heirs preserved the Dinsmore home, its furnishings, its papers and the supporting out-buildings and in 1988 conveyed them and 30 acres to the Dinsmore Foundation. It is listed on the National Register of Historic Places. Today it operates as a living museum.

The Dinsmore home, built in 1842.

The Dinsmore carriage house and privy.

This photograph shows the cooking cabin in the background. To the right is the back porch of the house. In the foreground is a grist stone from the Roberts mill. Note the steps leading up to the millstone. It was used by children to get onto their horses.

The Dinsmore wine making house.

The smokehouse.

CHAPTER EIGHT

THE LATER YEARS

A t the turn of the century Roberts was looking for new challenges. He turned 50 on October 4, 1901. He stopped his daily entries in his diary and instead wrote summarizations for each month. He purchased the telescope in Cincinnati and then immediately rented his farm to his brother-in-law Ben Cason. Except for grafting apple trees and planting them in his orchards, he doesn't mention farming anymore in his diary. He continued to build houses; builds a canning factory, a warehouse, the Belleview Baptist Church, and builds roofs on the Belleview Disciple Church and other buildings. He helped to install the first telephone lines and telephones in the area for the Woolper Telephone Co. in 1907. A few years later Middle Creek would become part of the Burlington, Middle Creek and Waterloo Telephone Co.[1] After March 1909, when Roberts wrote "Commenced keeping house alone in the shop" to work on the solar clock, there are no diary entries.

Ralph and Josephine Cason moved in the Roberts house in early 1913 and lived there continuously until Ralph's death in 1975. They raised their seven children in that home— Zora, Dorotha, Irene, Thelma (died at six months old), Luella, Betty Zane and Ivan. Roberts stayed active, still building houses and other structures. A record shows he was still building houses at age 73, shortly before his death.[2] Records also show he was still working on the roads in 1920 at age 69.[3]

Roberts slept in the upstairs bedroom in the swinging bed. He kept his organ in his bedroom, which he played until his death. He passed on his musical talents to his great-nieces and great-nephews. The five girls—Zora, Dorotha, Irene, Luella and Betty Zane-had a musical singing group for years that sang on the radio, at social gatherings, at weddings and the like. The children had a special relationship with their great-uncle, and all children had free roam of the house, even their Uncle Tom's bedroom. They were fond of his beard as it always had a bit of a wave to it. Every morning Roberts would go to the kitchen, pump up some water and wash his face in the ice-cold liquid.[4]

On March 16, 1917 Roberts sold his entire farm of 154 acres and house to Ralph Cason for $4,500.[5] On January 2, 1919 Roberts purchased 22 acres from Laura Belle Parson, which Roberts then sold to Ralph Cason shortly thereafter.[6] The yearly reunions in the Boone Cliffs hosted by Roberts continued well after his death. The reunions were a highlight of the year for the Roberts family as shown by the following newspaper article written by Roberts' brother-in-law Lafayette P. French in the *Boone County Recorder*:

BUFFALO.

There is no sickness at present.

The Sunday-school still prospers.

We have dry times in Buffalo, don't waste the water we hear on all sides.

The same old story here, the farmers are through their harvest and have gone to pressing hay and straw. Tom Roberts returned to his home in Boone County last Friday accompanied by L. P. French and family, to celebrate a family reunion at the old home on Middle creek. On our arrival we met some forty persons old and young who after hearty greetings separated to go climbing and scrambling over hills and cliff rocks. Near eleven o'clock we were called together for dinner assembling at the foot of a hill, where a little stream went babbling and dashing over cool mossy bolders and shinning pebbles. All partook of a bountiful repast and was it good, "It was." After dinner came the program for general entertainment. Prominent in our meeting was James Montgomery Roberts of Kansas City, Mo., and his accomplished wife. Mr. Roberts is a great grandson of Gen. W. H. Harrison and a cousin of ex-president, Benj. Harrison. Wm. Beasley and family, Poplar Bluff, Mo. Mrs. Ella Beasley claimed the right to say little but to feast her eyes on the dear faces she had not seen for so long and might never see again. Mrs. J. M. Roberts gave a talk on "Woman's Rights." Mrs. M. Cravens gave a talk. Closed by singing "God be with you till we meet again." We returned to the house and after refreshments and farewells some of parted never to all meet again on this side of the river of death.[7]

Roberts' death, like many things in his life, was not ordinary. In January of 1924 Roberts was found unconscious on the floor of the barn. He was carried to the house, and when he awoke, he got up and took his customary place at the dinner table. When the members of the family explained to him what had happened his only remark was something to the effect of "What a pleasant way to die."[8] His true feelings were disclosed in this prayer he wrote soon thereafter:

> Most Holy and Righteous God. I am thy creature though most unworthy. According to thy commandments I will pray for help and make a strong effort to live sincerely and purely before Thee. I implore Thee forget me not nor turn me away in my old age. Turn my heart to Thee and to Thy law. Give me of Thy strength for I am weak and sinful. Help my soul to praise and love Thee and to do Thy will I beg for Jesus sake.   January 25, 1924[9]

A year later Roberts was playing croquet with his grandniece Dorotha when he excused himself and went to the barn.

When he failed to come back Dorotha went looking for him and found him lying dead in the same place where he had been found a year earlier.[10] The *Boone County Recorder* reported his death:

> Quite a gloom was cast over a community last Thursday afternoon by the sudden death of one of our most highly honored citizens Mr. T.Z. Roberts of Middle Creek. [11]

His obituary was as follows:

Thomas Zane Roberts was found dead at his home on Middle Creek, Thursday evening, January 15th, at 4 o'clock in the afternoon. He had been attending to his usual duties all day Thursday and had no complaint to any of the family. He had suffered with shortness of breath and affection of the heart and this was no doubt, the cause of his death.

He was a consistent Christian and lived the life of his Master and Saviour as near as it was in his power to do. He was a student and genius, well versed in the Bible and its history, as well as in other good literature. He was a natural mechanic. One of his mechanical achievements was the building of a clock that not only recorded the time, but the moon changes, rising and setting of the sun and the day of the week and month. Mr. Roberts spent the greater part of his life farming, but he also taught school for a number of years. He did no man wrong.

The funeral service was held in Bellevue [now Belleview] Baptist Church, which was filled with his relatives and friends. He is survived by a brother, John Roberts, of Covington, and two sisters, Mary Cravens and Mrs. Ella Beasley, who are in California. He was never married.[12]

Ruth Kelly's recollections of Roberts are even more enlightening:

Mr. Roberts, as long as he lived, I'm sure he never stopped learning or studying. He was . . . what he didn't learn at school, why he taught himself. Because he studied everything and read. He wasn't a recluse or anything like that, or a hermit; he didn't live apart from the world. But he lived in the world but he really was not a part of it. I mean he never let it obsess his life or anything like that. He was a deep thinker and he thought a lot. He was a great student of nature. He commuted with nature, I know, all the time. That coupled along with his deep religious belief that he had was reflected in all. I don't imagine he was ever lonely in his life. Now, that's just the way he always impressed me. That he would never be lonely or bored because there would always be something he could find that would interest him. And I know he was a great reader. I don't think he minded being alone. He lived alone a lot of his life, and all. He was the type of man I think everybody respected. I never heard any harm of the man in my life.[13]

Roberts died on the same farm where he had been born and spent his entire life. His home, his solar clock, his swinging bed, his workshop and all the other monuments would remain another 50 years as his nephew Ralph Cason would act as caretaker until his own death. Roberts left the clock to Ralph Cason (valued at $35 in his estate) and the telescope to his nephew Hugh French (valued at $10 in the estate). When Ralph Cason died in May of 1975 the clock was still in its original sitting place. The lathe for building the clock and leftover cogs were still in the workshop. Cason had an open door policy at the Middle Creek home. Visitors were always welcome to come and see the clock and the home. There were annual school trips to the home from the area schools. People came from all over the U. S. and the world to see the clock, and Cason began a visitors log on June 24, 1934, which he kept until his death.

In 1993 the Cason family published a cookbook. The opening page states:

> "We dedicate this cookbook to the memory of Josie and Ralph Cason because of the way they opened their house . . ."

Roberts' grandniece Dorotha, who inherited Roberts' poetic abilities and has her own published book of poems, wrote this poem for the cookbook:

FOOD
The Cason family, through the ages
Has been know for fixin' food
Since we all seem to like to eat it
Especially when it tastes so good.

Folks always liked to come to our house
We always had good food to eat
Thru the summer we preserved it
In the winter quite a treat.

Preparing food takes time and energy
But you don't mind it not a bit
If when it's ready; folks enjoy it
Then you have made a great big hit.

To merit a compliment on your pie crust
Or even on lowly navy beans
Is such a good feeling you try even harder
To make it even better by any means.

If you want to make people happy
And a good way to make new friends
Fix some food and have them over
Play some games 'ere the evening ends.[14]

Upon Ralph Cason's death an era of Boone County history ended. The contents of the house were dispersed, some of it by auction. The clock was placed on loan to Northern Kentucky University for its science building for several years, then returned to a local Boone County bank in Burlington, the Heritage Bank, where it is presently on display in its lobby.

The preservation efforts in the Middle Creek valley started with The Nature Conservancy. On October 24, 1975 the Nature Conservancy purchased 46 acres of the Boone Cliffs.[15] On August 11, 1988 The Nature Conservancy enlarged the Boone County Cliffs Nature Preserve with the purchase of an additional 28.732 acres.[16]

On December 12, 1978 the Dinsmore heirs gifted 106.7 acres of the plantation to The Nature Conservancy.[17] A non-profit corporation was formed, the Dinsmore Homestead Foundation Inc., which purchased the Dinsmore homestead with the personal property and the other structures plus 30.7 acres from the Dinsmore heirs on May 27, 1988.[18] Earlier on December 28, 1987, Martha Breasted, a Dinsmore heir, had already gifted 78.7 acres to the foundation.[19] On December 31, 1987 the Dinsmore heirs sold 230.664 acres to the Boone County, Kentucky Public Properties Corporation.[20] This non-profit corporation sold 53.055 acres to the Dinsmore Homestead Foundation.[21] The remainder was used to establish the Middle Creek Park.

The Camargo Hunt Club, a fox hunting club, established itself in Boone County, Kentucky in the 1990s, although it had been in existence in Ohio since 1925.[22] Fox hunting has long been a tradition in the Middle Creek valley. The earliest issues of the *Boone County Recorder* in the 1870s and many thereafter report many large fox hunts in the Middle Creek area. In 2004 the Camargo Hunt Club sold 129 acres of its Boone County property in Middle Creek to the Boone Conservancy Inc., a non-profit corporation dedicated to the preservation of green space in Boone County.[23] The Boone Conservancy recently added a new purchase in 2005 of 44 acres of mine reclamation, which contains a large lake. [24] This addition will make over 600 acres of preserved property in the Middle Creek area.

The area has produced abundant wildlife. It is the home of whitetail deer, turkey, fox, and coyote as well as smaller animals. It is a favorite area for bird watching. Many notable artists have chosen this area as the subject of their talents. Caroline Williams, Tom Gaither, Pattie Purnell and Gary Akers have done paintings or drawings of the structures of Dinsmore. Michael DeMaria has done oil paintings of the Middle Creek General Store, which is still standing, as well as the Middle Creek Baptist Church and a rendition of a baptism in Middle Creek. Mary Amanda Moore has done several oil paintings of the Thomas Zane Roberts home. Undoubtedly there will be many more renderings to come as the preservation efforts of the Middle Creek valley continues.

Ralph Cason standing by the solar clock before his death in 1975.

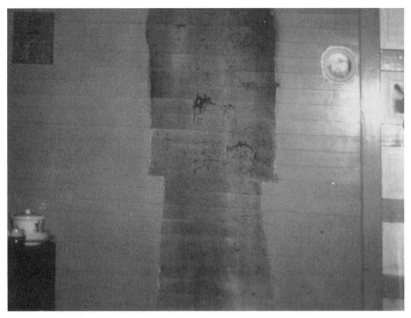

Photograph taken the day the clock was moved for the first time.
It was taken to Northern Kentucky University in 1975.
It was later moved to Heritage Bank and remains there.

This photograph was taken at one of the annual Roberts reunions at his home
in later years. Roberts is seated in the center.
Reunions were held at the Boone County Cliffs for many years.

The earliest newspaper articles show Middle Creek has long been a favorite place for fox hunting. Top picture shows Ralph Cason and fellow Middle Creek inhabitants. Left to Right: Ralph Cason, Jesse Louden Jr., Rafe "Bill" Koons, Wilbur Louden and Jesse Louden Sr.

Bottom picture shows the Camargo Hunt Club in action in Middle Creek. Photograph by William H. Chatfield, Esq.

The Boone County Cliffs are now owned by The Nature Conservancy, a national non-profit corporation, and is preserved as a park. The Cliffs are high conglomerate deposits left by glaciers 700,000 years ago and represent the finest glacial deposit in Kentucky.

The Middle Creek valley is still dotted with the remains of many old houses such as the one at right.

APPENDIX

THE WRITINGS OF ZANE

Thomas Zane Roberts was a poet, orator, author, and musician. Many of his poems and stories were published in the Boone County Recorder. He did not retain all of his writings. Most of what has been found has been through a process of looking through old newspapers. Many newspaper articles refer to the papers he read, or speeches he gave, but the documents themselves cannot be found. Some writings or pieces of music are in his handwriting in the justice of the peace book but are not published anywhere else. Other works of poetry and writings pasted in the justice of the peace book are suspected to have been written by Roberts. The poetry and writings provided in this appendix definitely were written by Roberts. Most of these writings were published in the Boone County Recorder. One unpublished poem provided in the appendix has been taken from the justice of the peace book. Although in rough form, it is still an enjoyable poem. The justice of the peace book contained other writings in rough draft form, but luckily Dorotha Griesser had finished versions in her possession. Some of these writings are provided in this appendix.

PENSEE

And Jesus, rising, said unto them:
"He that is innocent among you, let him cast the first stone at her."

Speaking kindly of the erring—those whose feet
Have tripped and stumbled at some great temptation.
Oh! do not stone them with condemning words,
Expressions of contempt or looks of scorn,
Until you backward throw the light of thought,
Searching in memory's chambers for each act
That lies half-hidden in oblivion's gloom.
Allow the truth to guide you in your search,
And if you hear from out the inner depths
No guilty conscience raise accusing cry,
Why, even then, speak kindly of the erring.
How soon may even you be overcome
By Satan's cunning snares? Temptation woes
May come upon you as they did on Job,
And you will not be strong enough to stand.

The Boone County Recorder
No. 14 Vol. 1
December 23, 1875
(Written for the Recorder.)

Zane.

IN THE DEPTHS
By Zane

Isn't it strange that mem'ry brings
Scenes of the past to view?
Things that have happened long ago,
Presented clear and true?

And high old times, almost forgot,
Because so old, you know,
Are found and polished up by thought
Until they fairly glow.

And still more wonderful to me,
That mem'ry should supply
Such peace to those who all their lives
Live so that they may die.

But if we live for self alone,
A black cloud seems to pour
On us regretful memories
Of many a misspent hour.

The Boone County Recorder
No. 17 Vol. 1
Thursday, January 13, 1876
(Written for the Recorder.)

BEWARE, BOYS!
By Zane

What ails that miserable man,
That once was such a gentleman?
Although he never put on airs,
He fell in a lady's snares
By marriage.

You see him always on the go,
Clippiteclip, and he, I know,
Wears leaky boots on rainy days;
All this was brought about, he says,
By marriage.

Look at him now with broken nose,
And see how ragged are his clothes;
A banged up hat without a brim,
Shows us what has disgusted him
With marriage.

Then boys, don't think of such a move,
As going to see or making love
To any lady in the land,
For fear that you might ask her hand
In marriage.

The Boone County Recorder
No. 19 Vol. 1
January 27, 1876
(Written for the Recorder.)

QUEER, BUT UNQUESTIONABLE
By Zane

On the top of a lofty hill in beloved Boone stands an old cottage. It is embowered in a cluster of dark green trees, whose cool shadows fall at noontide on a smooth sward of grass and flowers. Luxuriant vines twine round the columns of the porch, crowned with coronas of beautiful flowers, whose fragrance is often wafted by the gentle zephyr through the open window or the door ajar.

But the chief attraction of the old home is Bertie Spencer, whose beauty, accomplishments and good nature have made her—what is rarely found—the belle and the favorite of the neighborhood.

One evening, as she sat by the parlor window reading that last Recorder, and smiling over some of the quaint news items, she heard a step on the walk. To judge from the rosy tinge that mantled her cheek, one would suppose that she recognized that manly tread, but by what power of intuition I will leave to others to explain.

"Good evening, Miss Bertie," and the doorway is darkened by a tall, light complected, fine looking man of middle age, who doffs his hat gracefully.

"A pleasant evening to you, Mr. Abbott. Come in."

"My friend, Mr. Strebor," said Mr. Abbott, introducing his companion; and Bertie saw before her a dark whiskered, black-eyed man, whose face indicated cunning, if not power.

He seemed to be ill at ease, or, as we term it, bashful, at first; but under the influence of Bertie's pleasant smiles, he gained courage, and developed such a fund of information, anecdotes and traveling experiences as to become quite brilliant; which so delighted Bertie that she quite neglected Mr. Abbott in listening to him, causing the latter to frown fretfully.

"Suppose we have some music," said Abbott, by way of diversion, looking toward the organ.

"Yes; do, please," assented Mr. Strebor, as the young lady hesitated.

"With pleasure, if you two will assist me in singing."

Here again Mr. Abbott appeared at a disadvantage; for although a good bass singer, his friend's mellow tenor was captivating.

But a pleasant evening cannot last always, and, as they arose to go, Mr. Strebor remarked:

"It has been a long time since I have spent as pleasant an evening, Miss Spencer, and if, in the distant future, the shadows of adversity brood over me, the light of the happy time will cheer my soul, dispel the clouds, and encourage me to push forward to the land beyond the river."

"I hope it will, and that you will be a better man than Moses ever was," said Bertie with a smile.

"I hope Will has enjoyed himself," added Mr. Strebor; "though I suppose if he had been by Miss Laura's side he would have been supremely happy."

"It is evident you don't know what you are talking about," retorted Abbott. "Who gave you such an idea as that?"

"Your Royal Highness deigned to communicate your preference for her to your humble servant," said Strebor with mock humility.

"It is false; or rather you are mistaken, for-"

"Gentlemen," interrupted the lady, "there seems to be a misunderstanding about some trivial matter, but please let it pass. What does it matter? What difference does it make in a century or two?"

Mr. Strebor felt the rebuke and hung his head, but Abbott looked sternly revengeful.

"Look here, my friend; your conduct demands an explanation," said Will Abbott, as they rode from the house.

"In what way?"

"Why you have acted as though I was an enemy, instead of a friend," said Will, heatedly.

"Well, according to my last judgment, you are," coolly. "What would you think of a professed friend who tells the young ladies that you are indolent, dissipated and, above all, poor?"

"Why, I never said anything of the kind about you," affirmed the tall man with a look of astonishment on his face.

"Are you in earnest?" asked Ednor.

"Certainly. Can't you believe me?"

"Yes, and I am sorry for what has passed; and if you will accept the offer, I will prove my friendship by deeds," said Ednor, with apparent sincerity.

"I do accept it, with many thanks; and, as you are her friend, you can assist me very much if you will;" and all of Will's jealousy vanished.

"Why—well, I'll tell you how it is. I love Bertie Spencer, and I believe she likes me; and if you will speak a good work for me once in a while I believe she will say 'yes'."

"But, what if she says no?" asked Ednor turning away to hide a grin.

"Gracious! I hope she won't," ejaculated Will. "But if she does I'll tell her I was only joking."

Ednor's lip curled, but he only said, "I think I can influence her the right way," and with the usual compliments they separated.

Not long after this our friends again met at a party, when, as Mr. Abbott was busily engaged acting as Master of Ceremonies, Ednor found an opportunity to cross to where Miss Spencer was sitting. With a Chesterfieldian bow he took a seat by her side and said:

"It is with pleasure that I see you again, Miss Bertie."

"You probably say the same of the Zoo, or the Museum," smiled Bertie.

"Oh, pshaw, Miss Bertie, you know I—"

"N-o-i-s-e spells noise. Is that what you was going to say?"

"Do you see that man?" asked Ednor, pointing to Mr. Abbott.

Bertie shut her eyes and said, "No; who is it?"

"Why, Abbott," said Ednor.

"Where is the Abbess?" laughed the lady.

"Mr. Strebor looked at her a moment soberly. "Do you hear?"

"Tolerably well, thank you."

"I have something to tell you about him"

"Well, what is he about?"

"Shall I tell you here?"

"Why I can hear without you telling me to," said Bertie demurely.

"He thinks a great deal of you, and —"

"So does brother Charley," interrupted Bertie, the color slightly deepening in her cheeks.

"Yes, but you are his sweetheart."

"Did he tell you that I was sweet to his heart?"

"Yes," said Ednor.

"Then he is mistaken," said Bertie, repressing a tremor, "for if he had a sweetheart he would have given her his heart; and of course she couldn't be sweet to his heart if he had none."

"Powers of darkness! Won't you listen to me a moment?" asked Strebor in despair.

"Oh, well, you needn't swear at me, I won't talk to you if it vexes you," pouted Bertie, mischieviously.

"He says he is going to offer himself to you, and if you refuse him he'll call you a flirt, and say he was only joking."

"How loud will he call?" asked the lady carelessly; but her cheek paled, while her black eyes sparkled ominously.

Just then Mr. Strebor was called upon to take his place in the play, and Mr. Abbott, who was released, came up and inquired which she preferred, to take part or to take a stroll on the lawn.

"I am weary of the play," she said coldly; whereupon they passed out on the lawn, and after promenading to and fro a few times, took their seats on a rusty settee under the shade of a spreading elm.

The scenery from this point is beautiful. A winding valley coursed by a silver stream, stretches away toward the southwest, and the eye may follow the windings of the brook until they are lost in the filmy distance. Across the valley the tinkling cowbells chime a merry interlude as the lowing herd winds slowly o'er the tall hills, whose wooded summits tower high in the air. The slanting beams of the setting sun fall like a sheen of glory on Nature's foliate monuments, on the fields of green and gold, on the peasant's cottages, which latter looks as though painted in living light.

But to resume. As she sat looking out over the beautiful landscape, that same red light playing over her fine features and dancing in her dark eyes, Bertie Spencer looked dangerously beautiful.

"Miss Bertie, I will embrace the present opportunity to-to-in fact, Bertie, I love you, and that is a fact, and I ask you to be my wife," said Abbott, and in his earnestness he slipped from the settee, and was kneeling by her side, clasping her hand in both of his.

She blushed and trembled, and – but just then Mr. Strebor's words rang in her ears, and she said:

"Mr. Abbott, I am a flirt."

He looked at her a moment in sorrowful amazement, slowly rose to his feet, and said with a voice full of anguish, "God forgive you, Miss Spencer, for I never can."

"Ha! Ha! Ha!" laughed an unseen spectator; and the next moment, Mr. Ednor Strebor stood looking at him with a broad grin.

Light poured upon Mr. Abbott, and with it frenzied anger. "Traitor!" he hissed, as he sprang toward him.

With a sharp cry, Bertie started toward them, when a loud report pounded in her ears, followed by a keen pain in her arms, and she sank to the earth unconscious.

When the darkness cleared away from her dazed brain, she found herself lying surrounded by her friends, Laura and Daisy Neilson.

"What has happened? What have they done?" she inquired anxiously.

"How can we tell her?" said Laura with averted face.

"What is it?" Oh, do please tell!" she asked eagerly.

"Oh, it's only this, that Mr. Abbott was hurt in the fracas, and Mr. Strebor has fled, but I am sure he will be hung yet—and how does your arm feel darling?" said Daisy kindly.

"It is very painful. It is broken; is it not?"

"One bone only is broken," said Daisy, "and we are truly thankful you was [sic] not killed."

"Was Mr. Abbott badly hurt?"

The sisters exchanged glances of apprehension.

"Yes," said Laura, slowly, "they say he is mortally wounded. But it may be a mistake," she hastened to say, as she saw the anguish her announcement caused Bertie, "for---" someone's hurried approach interrupted her, and opening the door, Charley Spencer rushed into the room, and said hastily:

"Where is Bertie, and how is she?"

"I am doing very well; what is the news, Charley?"

"The worst is your getting hurt. The rest is not so bad as was first reported. Mr. Abbott received a flesh wound on the side, but with care will recover."

A few weeks after the foregoing incidents, Miss Bertie was going about with her arm in a sling, looking very interesting.

One evening as she walked arm in arm with Laura Nielson, at the house of the latter, a tall, distinguished-looking man rode up to the gate.

"Why, it is cousin Alfred!" cried Laura delightedly; as he advanced, met him with extended hand. "Miss Spencer, Mr. Nielson," and the tall man bowed gracefully.

Their acquaintanceship progressed rapidly, and as Bertie was very favorably impressed with his appearance at first, the impression was not at all weakened by his engaging manners.

So that when Mr. Abbott appeared on the arena, she had almost forgotten him, and all of his subsequent efforts to win back her wandering affections were in vain. He finally gave up in despair, muttering maledictions on the fair and the false one, and still lingers along the walk of life in single blessedness.

Ednor Strebor had left the county, and was living secluded in the fens and caves of the forest. Privation, fear, and remorse had had a salutary effect on him, and his was now a humble and contrite spirit. And with the change came a strong desire to see the old house at home, once more, even at the risk of detection and arrest. By traveling the night he had, unobserved, reached familiar scenes, when, one evening he was walking along an unfrequented road through the woods, he heard behind him the rapid approach of a carriage. He sprang into the bushes, and had scarcely secreted himself when he heard the occupant of the carriage cry for help. Humanity overcame every other consideration, and he ran out in the lane and started toward the traveler. A rough looking man held the horse while another was climbing into the carriage.

With a yell that would have done credit to a Commanche, Ednor charged down the road at full tilt. There was a hasty scramble from the wagon by one ruffian who fell head over heels into the ditch, while the other, drawing a revolver, fired a random shot at Ednor, which so frightened the horse that he leaped into the air, loosing the ruffian's hold on the bridle, throwing him down, and running the buggy over him. The shot, although fired hurriedly, took affect in Ednor's foot, bringing him to the ground. By a desperate effort he arose, seized the frightened horse as it passed, and succeeded in stopping it. As the assailants again started toward them, no time was to be lost. Ednor hopped to the carriage, climbed in and then fainted; but only for a moment, the air of the rapidly moving vehicle restoring his consciousness, and with it, the fierce pain of broken bones and mangled flesh.

"And is it really you Mr. Strebor?" said a familiar voice.

He looked up in astonishment that deepened into amazement, as he gazed into the sympathetic violet eyes of Laura Nielson. He dropped his eyes, and groaned with pain and shame.

"Yes, Miss Laura, it is I, and I suppose you will now deliver me to justice. Well, the sooner the better, for I am weary of my unworthy self, and long for a quiet rest in the grave."

Looking up quickly and seeing the expression of her countenance, he exclaimed eagerly:

"You have something to tell me? Speak; is it good news: Did they die?"

"Not by any means; for they are both well, that is, if you mean Miss Bertie and Mr. Abbott."

"Thank God! But then, that is no excuse for me, and I will try to make none," said Ednor, humbly.

"Here we are at last," said Laura, "and pa, John, and cousin Alfred shall help you into the house."

Ednor expostulated, "I would rather be taken home."

"We can take care of you," said Laura, decidedly; and that settled it.

The next day Mr. Alfred Nielson took Miss Bertie to church. On the way he told her of Laura's adventure, and said Mr. Strebor would like to see her.

"With great pleasure," said Bertie; "we will go right from church."

"By the way, did you know that Mr. Abbott drops in quite often, and that he and Miss Daisy promenade the lawn in the moonlight?" questioned Mr. Nielson, laughingly.

"Indeed?" surprised.

"Yes, and we will all meet there this evening. Won't we have a happy time? I never saw Laura look so happy as she did this morning," continued Mr. Nielson. "I rather think Mr. Strebor told her the old story last evening."

"I knew she liked him," said Bertie, "and his trouble went very hard with her; but now the golden bowl is full to overflowing with happiness for more than one," with a shy smile at her companion.

The Boone County Recorder
No. 20 Vol. 1
Thursday, February 3, 1876
(Written for the Recorder.)

PROFANITY
By Zane

How oft amid some festive scene,
When mirth seems gushing forth
From out the hearts of those we love,
Whose manners ought to be above
The low blasphemous oath.

We hear the Name of Mystery,
Immersed in flechered foam
Of foul corrupted language, tossed,
Coupled with frightfully prayers, across
The portals of the tomb.

E'en past perditions gloomy vail,
They pray the great I AM
To send their souls—and whey they rail,
Their words would make a demon quail,
While they are coolly calm.

Is it not profitless to take
The name of God in vain?
Is it not profitless to break
The law our great Jehovah spake,
When Sinia burned in flame?

Oh let me urge you cease to swear,
For you are doomed to die;
And if you ever wish to wear
A golden crown in Eden fair,
Use no profanity.

The Boone County Recorder
No. 21 Vol. 1
Thursday, February 10, 1876
(Written for the Recorder)

LOVE
By Zane

Love is infatuation
Or rather fascination;
Some call it adoration,
But in my estimation
It's simply dissipation.
`Tis not my vocation.
Just to define and station
The characterization
Of love. The situation
Of those in this location
Is mental aberration
Coupled with desperation
And my recommendation
To such is flagellation.
`Tis said procrastination,
Used with immoderation,
Cures this intoxication,
If so, go warn creation
To crawfish like the nation.

The Boone County Recorder
No. 23 Vol. 1
Thursday, February 24, 1876
(Written for the Recorder)

LIVELY STORIES FOR LIVELY FOLKS
First Paper
By Zane

Some time since, as I was walking along a shady lane with an old friend in the cool of a summer evening, he told me the following story:

One morning, a few years since, my brother and I concluded to "go a fishing", to endeavor to secure some of the finny treasures of the beautiful Ohio. After arming ourselves with all the necessary paraphernalia required to successfully pursue the science of angling, we started for the river. We went off in such a hurry as to forget to take a lunch with us, consequently, when evening came we had fine appetites, with nothing to satisfy them but a water-melon, which is, you know, to a hungry man merely, a great big nothing. Nevertheless, as we had had such fine luck hitherto (one little fish),we determined to stay all night. The night was warm, almost sultry, yet we built a small fire to give us light, and then we settled ourselves to watch for a "bite".

"Foolish idea," thinks I to myself, "why, the fish won't bite at night for they are probably asleep."

And so it seemed, for they didn't trouble us any that night. An old fisherman told us it was because the water was falling, but as I could not see the philosophy in it, I didn't believe it.

Getting weary of holding a perfectly inert line, I scrambled up the bank, stretched along the grass, under the dense foliage of a spreading maple, and was soon in the land of dreams.

How long I slept I have no means of knowing, but an unusual sound awoke me. I laid still, with my eyes shut, and listened. A dull, rumbling noise overhead reminded me of thunder, which supposition was still further strengthened by a few pattering drops in the leaves, while the pitchy darkness was fearful. (I had forgotten that my eyes were shut.) But, now the sound is like that of falling timber, and with a roar like Niagara, torrent a bursts through the leafy boughs and converts my bed into a lake instanter. I sprang to my feet and retreated through the bushes double geared, but had not proceded far until discovered that it had not rained in that particular spot, and, on looking up, beheld the stars shining! And on the heels of this discovery took the one that the water was deluging that one tree only.

I was standing on my head to let the water run out of my boots, when a shout from Dearna attracted my attention, or, rather, apprehension, and, starting toward him hastily, and rather carelessly, I was precipitated in a very unsafe manner over the bank. However, escaping without serious injury, I hastened to him, to find that he had enjoyed the same hydrostatic advantages as myself; for the water on the top of the bank had accumulated until it reached the sandy edge, when bursting over, it descended in a perfect torrent on our little camp, putting out the fire and leaving us wet and shivering in the dark.

Upon reconnoitering next morning among the scenes of the night's confusion, we discovered the singular cause of all our mishaps, viz: The tree-frogs had gnawed off a large grapevine, and the water came from the bleeding wound.

The Boone County Recorder
No. 24 Vol. 1
Thursday, March 2, 1876
(Written for the Recorder)

GRACIOUS ME!
By Zane
(Dedicated to his Friend Charley)

I'm going to say—
Now, what do you suppose?
I'm going to tell—
But what will I disclose?

I'll tell you now,
About what it will be,
And then you'll guess
What 'tis that aileth me.

Sometimes I eat,
And then again I don't
Sometimes I sleep,
And then again I won't.

Often I dream,
And often are they sweet;
At times in broad daylight
They can't be beat.

E'en when at work
Flowing the growing corn,
Awaiting hungrily
The sound of dinner horn.

Or, when with hoe
I grub the prickly thorn,
Watching the sun
Rise in the early morn.

Castles in air
I build with lavish hand;
Gigantic, and
The fairest in the land.

But why is it
That in my marble halls
A form intrudes,
Whose voice like music falls?

The form I know;
`Tis of a fair young girl;
Her silv'ry tones
Oft set my brain awhirl.

Sometimes I think
She loves, when—yes, just so—
Ah! now you'll say,
"He's dead in love, I know."

The Boone County Recorder
No. 33 Vol. 1
Thursday, May 4, 1876
(Written for the Recorder)

The editor of the *Boone County Recorder* wrote the following in the May 11, 1876 newspaper:

A certain young gentleman, who resides in a certain neighborhood not 100 miles from here was meandering about the County Clerk's office last Saturday, and when we take into consideration his contribution in this issue, his maneuvers look the more suspicious.

A TOTAL WRECK
Thursday, May the 11th, `76
To the Editor of the Recorder: SIR!

May a biting north wind always furnish you
      air!
May the hottest of sunshine just sizzle your
      hair!
May the door always stand in the way of
      your nose,
And a big, burly booby oft step on your toes!
      Sir `ee
      I would be
      Too rejoicing by half
To see you get crippled. Ha! Wouldn't I
      Laugh?

And this is the reason, you barbarous wit,
You did me a favor I don't like a bit.
You said in your paper (you've plenty of
      cheek)
That I went to the Clerk's office, Saturday
      week.
      Ah me!
      If a flea
      Could a cannibal be,
How gladly I'd see him just masticate thee!

When I went to see Della, on last Thursday
      eve,
And said, "Little darling, my heart please
      receive,"
Says she, "I have heard, sir, your license
      you've got,
You are in too much haste, sir, for I'd rather
      not!"

Heigh ho!
What a blow
To a fond heart like mine!
I'm spoiling this letter with optical brine.

And I say, Mr. Ed., that it's no laughing
matter,

With your brain in a whirl and your heart
in a clatter,
To see your dear girl with a bow leave the
room,
Then to jerk up your hat and dash away
home—
Boo-hoo!
And for you,
I think it's a sin,
In view of such sorrow to sit there and grin.

And now, Mr. Editor, what shall I do?
If a thorn or a pebble should get in my shoe
A person might think that the pain would
reveal it—
With my shattered nerves I scarcely can
feel it.
I know
'Tis a go,
And that never again,
Will peace twin a wreath for yours truly,
Poor Zane.

Thomas Zane Roberts

THE GOLDEN MORROW

By Zane

Respectfully dedicated to my valued friend, Mrs. M. S. Rice

Alone and weary in the dark
Cool shadows of the graveyard pines,
Beside the mossy stones which mark
The mansions of the dead, reclines
A mother in solemn reverie
Of those of hers who sleep beneath that tree.

With softened cadence comes the sound
Of distant cowboys' whistled strain;
And chirping crickets in the ground
Send lazy echoes back again.
But she, rapt list'ner, hears with ecstasy
A spirit voice, "Mother, we wait for thee."

"All, all is light, and joy, and love,
And gentle Jesus smiles to see
Thy children in the courts above
Dwell in such peaceful harmony.
Be sure and come to spend eternity
Where life is endless bliss; we wait for thee."

"Mother, for thee we sought the face
Of him who keeps the book of fate."
He smiled and said, "The loving grace
And saving power of Christ is great.
With heart o'erflowing with sweet melody,
We praise our Savior and we wait for thee."

The sun, deep crimsoned, sank to rest;
Night flung her mantle o'er the earth;
The stars were weeping for th' oppressed,
And lo! The dewdrop gems had birth.
The mother, homeward walking silently,
Still hears the whisper sweet, "We wait for thee."

The Boone County Recorder
No. 38 Vol. 1
Thursday, June 8, 1876

LIVELY STORIES FOR LIVELY FOLKS
Second Paper
By Zane

As I was standing headdownwards on anticipation, or in other words, expecting nothing, a few days since, who should I see but Dearna ride up to the gate! I hastened to extend the welcoming hand of hospitality, but he said, "You must excuse me, Zane, I am in some haste. I called to give you an invitation to a party on Maple Ridge to-night. I will look for you there." And galloping fleetly away he was soon lost to sight in the evening shadows which were even then falling.

Well, after what seemed an age of work and worry, hurrah and hurry, I succeeded in getting a start. Reaching the place at last, I sprang from my horse, rushed up to the house, knocked at the door and was warmly welcomed, or at least welcomely warmed, (for it was cold); and so much for preliminaries.

I jerked off my hat, bowed and said, "How are ye," to the people, and then with a desperate but vain effort to appear self-possessed, I succeeded in reaching a back seat; not one with a back, however, for I backed up against the wall. After an effort requiring real strength, coupled with a seeming desire to mash somebody's toes or kick the carpet off the floor, I succeeded in reaching the sofa, where Sally and Sam sat, saying "sweetest" softly, so suspiciously like sugary simpletons, and with her for a partner I dashed recklessly into the first play.

In the first and second plays I succeeded passably, only kissing one girl on the end of her nose, and another on the top of her head.

But in the third one—ah, me! how shall I tell it! Well, here goes:

It was a play called "Chasing the Squirrel," and after I saw the first couple go through the interwoven and mystic race, I began to be apprehensive of the result, but glancing over at my partner and seeing her composedly awaiting our time, I determined to do, and that daringly.

Well, our turn came at last and with palpitating heart, I started off after the "squirrel". Finding that the young lady was gaining ground, somewhat, I turned the corner the third time with a whiz. I heard a smothered scream of, "Oh, oh! he's mashed my toe," but I didn't stop to apologize, dashing away up the aisle after the nimblest piece of femininity that ever tripped a laughing race in that never-to-be-forgotten-play.

I thought I was recovering lost distance, somewhat, when one of the boys (may a one-eyed, three-legged, insane mosquito make away with him) stuck out his foot, and away I went across the room like a flying "squirrel", sure enough. As it happens, my sweet Della and the other young lady were sitting just in front of me and of course they were upset. Just then the hostess came in with a tray of cake and ice cream, and before I could arrest sufficient momentum ad terriblum to stop, we collided—chairs, girls, boys, old lady and all at the rate of forty miles per minute, and kerplash, rattle, crash, down came the ice cream all over my head and coat and down my back, making me think highly concentrated extracts of shivers and sneeze.

It is unnecessary to enter into a detailed account of how I got away— escaped. Suffice it to say that Della would not speak to me when I started home. Sad, sad!

The Boone County Recorder
No. 41 Vol. 1
Thursday, June 29, 1876
(Written for the Recorder)

LOOKOUT, ZANE!

To the Editor of the Recorder:

Respected Sir—I have hesitated some time about sending you this, even after Zane's repeated irritating allusions to me; but at last forbearance ceases to be a virtue, and, believing that you will kindly give me space in which to reply, I send this for publication. Hoping you will not think unmaidenly in thus coming before the public, I remain,

Yours sincerely,
Della

To Zane:
Sir, I am sorry you have said
So much respecting me;
It seems as if you wish to tread
Upon me ruthlessly.

What have I done that you should fling
Your scornful words so deep?
How many bitter tears they bring
To eyes that should not weep!

`Tis true I left you with a bow,
And took up your hat—
Had brother Jim been there, I know
He would have knocked you flat.

Zane, you remember what you said
That evening, there, to me.
`Twas, "Della, you and I will wed;
You're good enough for me."

"You're pretty tonguey, very sly,
And rather ugly, too;
But, on the whole, you fill my eye,
And so I'll marry you."

Were I as a brave, puissant man,
I know what I would do.
I'd tie you to a coal oil can,
And then I'd- scatter you.

Farewell. If ever you should come
Around this way again,
I'll make my father drive you home,
You foppish, foolish Zane.

The Boone County Recorder
No. 42 Vol. 1
Thursday, July 6, 1876
(Written for the Recorder)

POOR ZANE.

(We receive the following valediction from "Zane". Reader, draw your own inference—Ed.)

To the Editor of the Recorder:
        Sir, if I was not so lazy,
        I would certainly go crazy,
        For my wits feel very sleazy,
And I shiver with a quiver at the sound
        At the biting tones of Della,
        When she says: "You git, you fellah!"
        How I snatched up my umbrella!
And like lightning with a whit'ning face I bound
        Out the door and o'er the fences.
        What care I for cash expenses,
        So I reach secure defenses,
When I'm resting, no molesting gals around.

        Whoop, hurrah! but ain't I lucky,
        And I rather think I'm plucky,
        But I'll wend no more that mucky,
Muddy, meiry, sticky, wiry road again;
        For with a dream of love exploded,
        And to raving maddness goaded,
        With this pistol double loaded,
I will ever and forever end my pain.

        Heavens, there's that bloody dripping,
        Pallid ghoul toward me tripping.
        With hot pinchers it is ripping,
Tearing, breaking, hissing, raking through my brain!
        Horror! Here's a demon roaring
        With a blazing auger boring
        Deep into my spinal coring—
Farewell mother, soon—.

The Boone County Recorder
No. 43 Vol. 1
Thursday, July 13, 1876
(Written for the Recorder)

SENSATIONS OF A SUICIDE.

To the Editor of the Recorder:

Sir—The following blank verse portrays the Nervous phenomena attendant upon the reception of a good pistol ball, which passed through the right lobe of the cerebrum and out at the expansion of the skull over the volitive region, from the effects of which I am slowly recovering.

Yours, Zane.

A crash of a world in fragments riven,
And pain of a soul in tortured chaine,
While helveless lancets, hurled at wondrous speed,
By force electric, pierced me through and through.
Alternate flames and freezes compassed me,
Holding high carnival in altercative rage.
The former, with a seeming merry malice,
Came dancing o'er me with their scorching feet,
And shaking hand with every quivering nerve,
They formed themselves into a hissing riot
Of howling demons. With disruptive bars,
Prospecting for the papillae, they tore
The flesh from off my mangled skeleton,
And then dissolved in suffocating smoke.

Then came the freezing form of gaunt despair,
With grim destruction looking o'er his shoulder,
Numbing my bones as they reclined unfleshed.
Yet, still advancing with exultant strides,
They fell upon me—tore me from limb to limb—
Then casting icy darkness o'er me,
They left me hopeless, soulless, and alone.

    *   *   *   *

A glim'ring light, a glancing ray,
    `Tis here—`tis gone—so very bright,
Me thought it was the dawn of day,
    Swift breaking through the night.
Was it the light of blazing torch
    Held by a loving angel hand?
And are they waiting at the porch
    To take me by the hand?

Ah, no! `Tis here; `tis cold, `tis gray,
    And with its pulsing wave of pain,
While seeming spirits softly say,
    "Thank God, he'll live again!"

The Boone County Recorder
No. 48 Vol. 1
Thursday, August 17, 1876
(Written for the Recorder)

A MODERN HUSBAND
By Zane

I've had a splendid trade to-day,
    Made fifty dollars clear, I know:
'Twas Jenny's horse I swapped away,
And likely she will cry and say,
    "Husband, I'll miss him so!"

But what are woman's tears to dismiss,
    When we must have our bread and meat.
They say I'm rich, but then the times
Are hard. To-day I sued Jake Grimes
    For that one stone of wheat.

But here I am at home again—
    Jo-Jo, come here and shut this gate!
Put up this horse! And where is Ben?
He said he'd be at home by ten—
    Why is he out so late?

Bring up the horsewhip from the barn;
    I'll teach him how to see his girl!
He's ruining the whole consarn
With loving that poor Edna Varhn,
    I'll settle him, the churl!

Here, wife, get up and stir around;
    I want some supper, fresh and hot;
"Not well? All in the safe?" Confound
A woman always so unsound
    A worthless wife I've got!

Don't "Husband" one, I hate to see
      You always sniffling baby tears;
Here's Ben. Jo, bring that whip to me,
Jenny, go `way and let me be—
      Woman, I'll box your ears!
I'll let you off, "sweet honey spark,"
      For just this once; but if you stay
Out once again till after dark,
Or if you're not up with the lark,
      I'll teach you the old way.

Bring up the stand and let's to prayers.
      "Too late?" No, not by the half it ain't.
Wake up that girl from off the stairs,
We'll go to bed; come, dry your tears,
      Jenny, you'd vex a saint.

The Boone County Recorder
No. 5 Vol. 2
Thursday, October 26, 1876
(Written for the Recorder)

The following poem was written in the justice of the peace book.

The first is Dump Marshall so pleasant of face
Though always so gracious, He's out of all grace
With dashing young ladies. The next – Robert Clore
Who likes his fast horses as well as before
And Tommie his brother (I pity thee boy)
Has a rattling sweet wife and a big baby joy
And Harry C. Botts is a regular stunner
With his four story shoes turned up like a runner
He is wondrously witty and wretched and wild
And wholly wrapped up in Miss (won'tell) dear child
And there's the dear doctor Piatt full of shill
But pericarditis does baffle him still
And Benjamin Corbin is Bass but not base
But his girl loving alive is seen in his face
The next Henry Clore, He that spreads out—away
Over there on the hilltop, He's lightening they say
And there's Bettie Acra and Miss Lucy Rice
Sure 25 billion would be a small price
If they could be bought. But let that suffice.
There's T Z Roberts who's always too late
He has six cords of wood stored away as his fate.
Oh Girls say him may whatever befall
For sure he would take you point pullbacks and all
Here's Jessey and Bobby and William and Will
And Jimmy and Andrew, a Bohemian still
And lots of the smaller fry come at the call
So come and be welcome there's wide room for all
We're rough but we're ready to join hand to hand
And march with our cross for the bright Happy land FAR AWAY

This poem written by Zane was in the possession of Dorotha Greisser.

Childhood Hours

Sometimes in summers golden time
When gentle zephers kiss the flowers
Then flaunt away—a perfumed clime
Of happy sunny hours

I wish I was a child again
As happy as in Days of yore
I gathered flowers in the glen
Or rambled o`er the moore

When in the tall trees of the wood
The feathered songsters of the wild
Are warbling notes and chasing food
So active, noisy, mild.

When in the dewy blush of morn
The larks sweet rondelay I hear
And far away the mellow horn
Falls softly on the ear

Or in the darkling shades of night
The wild dove mourns in travail
While high o`er all of pervious light
The tweetering swallows sail

How oft as pensively here I stay
Where flowery paths lead through the wild
I wish while wandering on my way
To be once more a child.

Zane

Chapter One:
The Solar Clock

1. There are numerous newspaper and magazine articles repeating the myth. Examples are: a. J.M. Huckabee, "A Horologist's Notes: Uncle Tom's Cabin…A Glimpse at His Diary", *American Horologist and Jeweler* June 1969: 48 and b. Kathy Perkins, "Uncle Tom's Clock," *N. KY Innerviews* Aug.-Sept. 1975.
2. Dorotha Greisser, "The Story of the Clock", Jack Ramey, "Rare Clock", *The Enquirer*, 9 May 1954.
3. Josephine Cason, "The Life of Thomas Zane Roberts" 10.
4. William I. Milham, *Time and Timepieces* (New York: The MacMillan Co., 1942) 351.
5. Dorotha Greisser, "The Story of the Clock", 4.
6. Ralph Cason, personal interview 1975.
7. Ruth Kelly, personal interview July 9, 1976.
8. Dorotha Greisser, "The Story of the Clock", 4. Ralph Cason reiterated this fact in personal interviews in 1975.
9. Ruth Kelly, personal interview July 9, 1976.
10. Howard McGehey, "Clock Built by Late Boone County Inventor Shows Movement".
11. Josephine Cason, "The Life of Thomas Zane Roberts" 11.
12. J.M. Huckabee, "A Horologist's Notes: Uncle Tom's Cabin…A Glimpse at His Diary", *American Horologist and Jeweler,* June 1969: 50. This story was reiterated by Ralph Cason in personal interviews in 1975.
13. J.M. Huckabee, 50.
14. Ralph Cason, personal interview 1975.
15. Ralph Cason, personal interview 1975.
16. Josephine Cason, 13.

Chapter Two:
Arrival in Boone County

1. William Conrad (Editor), *Boone County: The Top of Kentucky 1792-1992* (KY: Picture This! Books, 1992).
2. Cave Johnson, Autobiography of Cave Johnson, 1845. Boone County Clerks Records, Order Book A page 1.
3. Michael Capek, *Lively Stones: A Narrative History of The Belleview Baptist Church 1803-2003* (Tenn.: Tennessee Valley Publishing, 2002). 13, 14.
4. Paul Tanner, "A Brief History of Boone Circuit Court Burlington, KY 1805- 1933" 1.
5. R. Whitney Tucker, *The Descendants of The Presidents* (Charlotte, N.C.: Delmor Printing Company, 1975) 82.
6. Frances Bazley Lee, *Genealogical and Memorial History of the State of New Jersey* (Lewis Historical Publishing Company, 1910) 650.
7. John U. Salt, *The Daily Times Star,* "Hand Made Wonder Clock of Boone County Hills" Kentucky Edition, 19 October 1928, Page 9 Col. 3, 4.
8. Sigman Byrd, *The Kentucky Post and The Times Star* "Boone's World Clock… A 56 Year Marvel," 8 March 1969, front page.

9. Frank Gruber, *Zane Grey: A Biography* (Cleveland, OH: The World Publishing Company, 1970) 4.
10. Zane Grey, *The Spirit of The Border* (Rosalyn, N.Y.: Walter J. Black Inc., 1906) 3.
11. Jeff Carskadden and James Morton, *Where the Frolics and War Dances Are Held: The Indian Wars and The Early European Exploration and Settlement of Muskingum County and The Central Muskingum Valley* (Baltimore: Gateway Press, 1997) 364.
12. William Huntzen and Joseph Roxby, *The Tales of Wheeling's Frontier Era Heroic Age* (Apollo, PA: Clossom Press, 2000) 11-34.
13. John Drury, "The National Road," *Midwest Heritage* (1948) 101-110.
14. J.F. Everhart, *The History of Muskingum County, Ohio* (Columbus, OH: J.F. Everhart & Co., 1882) 7-8.
15. General Robert P. Kennedy, " Isaac Zane: The White Eagle of The Wyandots," *The Ohio Magazine,* Vol. 2 No. 1 (January 1, 1907) 295-300.
16. Martin, Myra N. *My Zane Lineage,* Waverly, Illinois, Feb. 24, 1964. Library of Congress, Washington D.C. Call No. CS 71.728 Volume 84/3173 Microfilm.
17. Martha Zane Roberts, The Gravestone of Martha Zane Roberts, IOOF Cemetery, Carrollton, Ky.
18. *Biographical Encyclopedia of New Jersey of The Nineteenth Century* (Philadelphia: Galaxy Publishing Company, 1877) 44; Beverly W. Bond Jr., *The Intimate Letters of John Cleves Symmes and His Family,* (Cincinnati, Ohio: Historical and Philosophical Society of Ohio) xxiii; Alta Harvey Heiser, *West to Ohio,* (Yellow Springs, Ohio: The Antioch Press, 1954) 134.
19. Jim Blount, FLASHBACKS: *Historical Vignettes About People Places and Events in Hamilton and Butler County, Ohio,* Volume One (Hamilton, Ohio; Past/Present/Press, 1995) 6.
20. Jim Blount, *Rossville: Hamilton's West Bank,* (Hamilton, Ohio: Past/Present/Press, 1994) 16.
21. Butler County Clerk's Records: Deed Book Z Page 226.
22. Jim Blount, *Rossville: Hamilton's West Bank,* 7.
23. Roxanna Odell Roberts, *Roberts Family Bible.*
24. *The Carrollton Democrat,* 27 May 1868, Vol. No. 10 Page 4; US Census Records 1860.
25. *The Carrollton Democrat,* 16 July 1870, Vol. III No. 16 Page 3 Col. 2.
26. Boone County Clerk's Records: Marriage Book B Page 31.
27. Jennifer S. Warner, *Boone County, From Mastodons to The Millennium (Ky: Boone County Bicentennial Committee, 1998)* 34.
28. Boone County Clerk's Records: Marriage Book D Page 31.
29. U.S. Census Records: 1870, for Trail Creek, Harrison County, Missouri.
30. *Marion Record* Volume XXXII No. 3, November 15, 1901 Page 1 Col. 2.
31. *A History and Biographical Encyclopedia of Butler County, Ohio* (Evansville, Indiana: Unigraphic Inc., 1971, facsimile of 1882 edition) 346-356.
32. *The Carrollton Democrat,* 16 May 1885, Vol. 28 No. 5 Page 5.

33. *Marion Record* Volume XXXIV No. 32, June 2, 1904 Page 1 Col. 5. The names and information are from U.S. Census records.
34. William Conrad, *Boone County 175th Anniversary Historical Book* 44.
35. Matthew Becher, *Images of America: Burlington* 75.
36. Caroline Williams, "A Spot Near Cincinnati", *The Enquirer*. January 25, 1848, 6.
37. Boone County Clerk's Records Deed Book O Page 48 and Boone County Clerk's Records Deed Book O Page 428.
38. Boone County Clerk's Records Deed Book N Page 217.
39. Boone County Clerk's Records Deed Book R Page 227.
40. William Conrad, *Boone County 175th Anniversary Historical Book* 29.
41. Mastadons to Millenium p. 51.
42. A.M. Yealey, *History of Boone County, Kentucky*, (Covington, Ky: Holmes High School Press, 1960)18.
43. Boone County Clerk's Records Deed Book O Page 552.
44. Boone County Clerk's Records Deed Book Q Page 282.
45. Boone County Clerk's Records Deed Book 28 Page 558.
46. U.S. Nonpopulation Census 1850.
47. Paul Tanner, "Slavery in Boone County, Kentucky and Its Aftermath," Oct. 1986.
48. Michael Capek wrote an excellent work in this area on Middle Creek Baptist Church members fighting in the Civil War in *Lively Stones: A Narrative History of the History of The Belleview Baptist Church*. John O. Roberts is mentioned in a newspaper article in the context of Civil War Veterans in *The Boone County Recorder* March 20, 1907.
49. *The Boone County Recorder,* November 30, 1876 Vol. 2 No. 10, Page 3 Col. 4.
50. *The Boone County Recorder,* Vol. 2 No. 11, 7 December 1876, Page 3 Col. 2.

Chapter Three:
T.Z.

1. Josephine Cason, "The Life of Thomas Zane Roberts" 10.
2. Josephine Cason, 9.
3. Dorotha Greisser, "The Story of The Clock", 1 Michael Capek, *Lively Stones: A Narrative History of The Belleview Baptist Church 1803-2003* (Tenn.: Tennessee Valley Publishing, 2002) 65.
4. Thomas D. Clark, *The History of Kentucky* (New York: Prentice–Hall Inc., 1937) 566.
5. Josephine Cason, 4.
6. *The Boone County Recorder,* Vol. 1 No. 15, December 30, 1875.
7. Michael Capek, 79.
8. Josephine Cason, 1.
9. Josephine Cason, 5.
10. Interviews with Ralph Cason, 1975.
11. *The Boone County Recorder,* Vol. 2 No. 34, May 17, 1877.
12. *The Boone County Recorder,* Vol. 5 No. 30, May 6, 1880.
13. Josephine Cason, 6.
14. Interviews with Ruth Kelly, July 9, 1976.

Chapter Four:
Middle Creek Baptist Church

1. *Michael Capek, Lively Stones: A Narrative History of The Belleview Baptist Church 1803-2003* (Tenn.: Tennessee Valley Publishing, 2002) 4.
2. William Conrad (Editor), *Boone County: The Top of Kentucky 1792-1992* (Ky: Picture This! Books, 1992) 3.
3. Michael Capek, 5.
4. The Church of Christ at Middle Creek Constitution.
5. Michael Capek, 8.
6. S.P. Brady, "The History of Middle Creek Church" (1874).
7. S.P. Brady, 5.
8. S.P. Brady, 5.
9. S.P. Brady, 6.
10. S.P. Brady, 7.
11. *Daily Recorder*, September 7-9, 1887.
12. *The Boone County Recorder,* Vol. 1 No. 41 29 June 1876, Page 3 Col. 2.
13. *The Boone County Recorder,* October 28, 1876.
14. William Conrad, 3.
15. William Conrad, 3.
16. William Conrad, 3.
17. Jennifer S. Warner, *Boone County, From Mastadons to The Millennium (KY: Boone County Bicentennial Committee)* 149.
18. S.P. Brady, 12.
19. Michael Capek, *The Minutes of Belleview Baptist Church* (September 1877).
20. Boone County Clerk's Records: Deed Book 30 Page 470.
21. Boone County Clerk's Records: Deed Book 30 Page 259.
22. *The Minutes of Belleview Baptist Church,* September 12, 1885.
23. Josephine Cason, 4.

Chapter Five:
Professor Roberts

1. William Conrad (Editor), Boone County: *The Top of Kentucky 1792-1992* (Ky: Picture This! Books 1992) 3.
2. William Conrad, 3.
3. William Conrad, "The History of Boone County Schools", 19.
4. William Conrad, "The History of Boone County Schools", 3.
5. *Boone County 175th Anniversary Historical Book 1798-1973,* 38.
6. *Boone County 175th Anniversary Historical Book 1798-1973,* 38.
7. *Boone County Recorder,* Vol. 2 No. 10, 30 November 1876.

8. Josephine Cason, 2.
9. William Conrad, "The History of Boone County Schools", 15.
10. *Boone County Recorder,* 22 August 1878.
11. *Burlington Advertiser,* 13 October 1849.
12. Josephine Cason, 2.
13. *Boone County Recorder,* Vol. 1 No. 1, 23 September 1875.
14. *Boone County Recorder,* Vol. 38 No. 44, 31 July 1913.
15. *Boone County Recorder,* 23 September 1875.
16. Josephine Cason, 4.
17. *Boone County Recorder,* 17 August 1876.
18. *Boone County Recorder,* 14 December 1876
19. *Boone County Recorder,* 29 November 1876.
20. *Boone County Recorder,* 6 December 1877.
21. *Boone County Recorder,* 13 December 1877
22. *Boone County Recorder,* Vol. 2 No. 20, 8 February 1877.
23. *Boone County Recorder,* Vol. 6 No. 46, 1 September 1881.
24. *Boone County Recorder,* 7 August 1889.
25. Dallas Howard Norris, "The Reorganization of The Boone County School System," University of Cincinnati, Thesis 18.
26. *Boone County Recorder,* 15 August 1878.
27. Dallas Howard Norris, 23.
28. *Boone County Recorder,* 25 August 1878.
29. *Boone County Recorder,* Vol. 3 No. 47, 22 August 1878.
30. Josephine Cason, 4.
31. Ruth Kelly, personal interview July 9, 1976.
32. *Boone County Recorder,* 26 August 1885.
33. Ralph Cason, personal interview 1975.
34. Ruth Kelly, personal interview July 9, 1976.
35. *Boone County Recorder,* 24 August 1876.
36. *Boone County Recorder,* Vol. 1 No. 26, 16 March 1876.
37. *Boone County Recorder,* Vol. 3 No. 50, 12 September 1878.
38. *Boone County Recorder,* 13 March 1913.
39. Paul Tanner, "Slavery in Boone County, Kentucky and Its Aftermath" 23-25.
40. *Boone County Recorder,* 2 September 1896.
41. *Boone County Recorder,* 27 January 1897.
42. *Boone County Recorder,* 24 August 1892.
43. *Boone County Recorder,* Vol. 37 No. 44, 20 August 1902.

Chapter Six:
Life On Middle Creek

1. William Conrad, "A Journey Into The Past"; *Boone County Recorder,* Historical Edition. Supplement to the *Boone County Recorder.*Thursday, September 4, 1930, p. 26; *Boone County Recorder,* October 8, 1902, page 4, col. 3; *Boone County Recorder,* October 15, 1902, page 5, col. 2.
2. *Boone County Recorder,* examples of neighborhood names are:
  a. "Reynardsburg" Vol. 1 No. 20, 30 September 1875.
  b. "Milling Valley" Vol. 1 No. 1, 23 September 1875.
  c. "Waterloo", Vol. 1 No. 35, 18 May 1876.
  d. "Wayside Gleanings", 23 October 1913.
  e. "Commissary", 4 December 1907.
  f. News about Julia Dinsmore (Dinsmore Plantation), John Bruce (Bruce's Middle Creek Grist Mill), Ben Cason (Roberts' Brother-in-law and farm near Roberts) and Will Walton (Walton's hill above Middle Creek Valley) are all listed in Reynardsburg News. (Vol. 1 No. 21, 10 February 1876; Vol. 1 No. 2, 30 September 1876; Vol. 2 No. 10, 30 November 1876). John Cox, who bought some of the Roberts farm, is listed under the Waterloo neighborhood Vol. 1 No. 34, 11 May 1876. Roberts farm was between the two areas.
3. Boone County Clerk's Records: Deed Book 30 Page 25.
4. *Boone County Recorder,* Vol. 3 No. 8, 15 November 1877.
5. Josephine Cason, "The Life of Thomas Zane Roberts" 8.
6. Dorotha Greisser, personal interview, June 19, 2006
7. These examples are taken from Roberts' diary.
8. Josephine Cason, "The Life of Thomas Zane Roberts" 9.
9. Thomas D. Clark, *The History of Kentucky* (New York: Prentice Hall Inc., 1937) 564, 587.
10. *Boone County Recorder,* 11 January 1876.
11. *Boone County Recorder,* 9 August 1877.
12. *Boone County Recorder,* 15 August 1878.
13. Thomas Zane Roberts, Diary, May 1906.
14. Thomas Zane Roberts, Diary, June 1906.
15. *Boone County Recorder,* Vol. 32, 24 April 1907.
16. *Boone County Recorder,* Vol. 32 No. 29, 8 May 1907.
17. Ruth Kelly, Personal Interview 9, July 1976.
18. Jennifer S. Warner, *Boone County, From Mastodons to the Millennium (Ky: Boone County Bicentennial Committee)* 92.
19. *Boone County Recorder,* Vol. 1 No. 22, 17 February 1876.
20. *Boone County Recorder,* Vol. 1 No. 1, 23 September 1875.
21. *Boone County Recorder,* Vol. 1, 27 January 1876.
22. *Boone County Recorder,* Vol. 1, 23 March 1876.
23. *Boone County Recorder,* No. 2, 23 February 1876.
24. *Boone County Recorder,* Vol. 1 No. 26, 16 March 1876.
25. Jennifer Warner, 128.
26. *Boone County Recorder,* Vol. 2 No. 2, 5 October 1876.
27. *Boone County Recorder,* Vol. 2 No. 4, 19 October 1876.
28. *Boone County Recorder,* Vol. 2 No. 10, 30 November 1876.
29. *Boone County Recorder,* Vol. 2 No. 11, 7 December 1876.
30. *Boone County Recorder,* Vol. 2 No. 35, 24 May 1877.
31. Jennifer Warner; *Boone County Recorder,* Vol. 3 No. 6, 1 November 1877.

32. *Boone County Recorder,* Vol. 28 No. 9, 17 December 1902.

33. *Boone County Recorder,* Vol. 38 No. 21, 2 February 1913.

34. *Boone County Recorder,* 23 October 1913.

35. *Boone County Recorder,* 20 November 1913.

36. *An Atlas of Boone, Kenton, and Campbell Counties, Kentucky 1883* (Philadelphia: D.J. Lake & Co. 1883) 15.

37. *Boone County Recorder,* Vol. 1 No. 28, 3 March 1876.

38. Jim Reis, *Pieces of The Past* (Ky.: The Kentucky Post 1988) 72, 246; Jennifer Warren, 71.

Chapter Seven:
The Dinsmore Middle Creek Plantation

1. Dinsmore Homestead Foundation, "Basic History of The Dinsmore Foundation," August 1990.

2. Silas Dinsmoor Papers #1717, James Dinsmore to Silas Dinsmoor, 23 June 1834 (Hanover, N.H.: Dartmouth College Baker Memorial Library Archives Dept.).

3. Boone County Clerk's Records: Deed Book M Page 26.

4. Ralph Cason, Personal Interview 1975, reaffirmed by Dorothy Greisser personal interviews, June 19, 2006.

5. Thomas Zane Roberts, *Diary.*

6. Boone County Clerk's Records: Deed Book 32 Page 83, October 11, 1880.

7. Michael Capek, *Lively Stones: A Narrative History of The Belleview Baptist Church 1803-2003* (Tenn.: Tennessee Valley Publishing, 2002) 48.

8. James Dinsmore letter to Silas Dinsmoor, February 1840.

9. *Covington Journal,* 26 October 1849.

10. William Conrad, "A Journey Into The Past".

11. *Boone County Recorder,* Vol. 1 No. 2, 9 December 1875.

12. Viola M. (Horton) Clore, *The Clore Family History* (Published by author 1980) 22.

13. Jennifer S. Warner, Boone County, *From Mastodons to the Millennium* (Ky.: Boone County Bicentennial Committee) 148; Dinsmore Homestead Foundation 11.

14. *Boone County Recorder,* Vol. 38 No. 1, 17 April 1913.

15. *Boone County Recorder,* Vol. 32 No. 31, 22 May 1907.

Chapter Eight:
The Later Years

1. *Boone County Recorder,* 8 January 1914.

2. Thomas Zane Roberts, "Letter to Earnest McNeely" 4 August 1924.

3. Ralph Cason, Road Work Records (possession of author).

4. Dorotha Greisser, personal interviews, Feb. 23, 2005.

5. Boone County Clerk's Records: Deed Book 59 Page 26.

6. Boone County Clerk's Records: Deed Book 61 Page 226.

7. *Boone County Recorder,* 1 August 1894. Buffalo refers to an area around present day Union, Ky.

8. Ralph Cason, personal interview, 1975.

9. Thomas Zane Roberts, Diary.

10. Ralph Cason, personal interview; Dorotha Greisser, personal interviews, 23 February 2005.

11. *Boone County Recorder,* 22 January 1925. Vol. 49, No. 12, p. 6.

12. *Boone County Recorder,* 28 January 1925.

13. Ruth Kelly, personal interview 9 July 1976.

14. Cason Family, *Timeless Recipes,* (Tenn.: Fundcraft Publishing, 1993).

15. Boone County Clerk's Records: Deed Book 391 Page 47.

16. Boone County Clerk's Records: Deed Book 254 Page 190.

17. Boone County Clerk's Records: Deed Book 387 Page 45.

18. Boone County Clerk's Records: Deed Book 387 Page 45.

19. Boone County Clerk's Records: Deed Book 378 Page 154.

20. Boone County Clerk's Records: Deed Book 378 Page 265.

21. Boone County Clerk's Records: Deed Book 568 Page 245

22. William H. Chatfield, *The Camargo Hunt Club* (Ohio: The C.J. Krekbriel Company, 2001) VII.

23. Boone County Clerk's Records: Deed Book 876 Page 440 & Boone County Clerk's Records: Deed Book 876 Page 444.

24. Boone County Clerks Records: Deed Book 908 Page 215; Luke Saladin, "From Pit to Park," *The Kentucky Post,* March 7, 2006.

BIBLIOGRAPHY

A History and Biographical Encyclopedia of Butler County, Ohio. (Evansville, Indiana: Unigraphic Inc. 1971, facsimile of 1882 edition) 346-356.

An Atlas of Boone, Kenton, and Campbell Counties, Kentucky 1883. Philadelphia: D.J. Lake & Co. 1883.

Barnes, Judi. "Natural Adventure at Boone Cliffs," *Dixie News,* 23 November1977.

Becher, Matthew E., Michael D. Rouse, Robert Schrage, & Louise Wilcox. *Images of America: Burlington.* Great Britain: Arcadia Publishing, 2004.

Bell, Carol Willsey. *Ohio Wills and Estates to 1850: An Index,* Youngstown, Ohio: Bell Books, 1981.

Biographical Encyclopedia of New Jersey of The Nineteenth Century. Philadelphia: Galaxy Publishing Company,1877.

Blincoe, Caden. Down at Dinsmore. Ky.: Picture This Books, 1991.

Blount, Jim. FLASHBACKS: Historical Vignettes About People and Places in Hamilton and Butler County, Ohio. Hamilton, Ohio: Past/Present/Press, 1995.

Blount, Jim. Rossville: Hamilton's West Bank. Hamilton, Ohio: Past/Present/Press, 1995.

Bond, Beverly W. Jr. The Intimate Letters of John Cleves Symmes and His Family. Cincinnati, Ohio: Historical and Philosophical Society of Ohio, 1956.

Boone County Clerk's Records. Burlington, Ky.

Boone County Historic Review Board. *Historic Structures of Boone County, Kentucky.* Michigan: Cushing-Mallory, Inc., 2002.

Boone County 175th Anniversary Historical Book 1798-1973.

Boone County Planning Commission. *Western Boone County Study 1998.* Burlington: Kentucky, 1998.

Boone County Recorder newspaper. Florence, Ky.

Bradford, Thomas G. *Map of Kentucky.* 1838 Somerset, Ky.: Reproduced by Art Reproductions, LLC.

Brady, S.P. "The History of Middle Creek Church," 1803-1874.

Byrd, Sigman. "Boone's World Clock... A 56 Year Marvel. *The Kentucky Post and Times Star.* 8 March 1969. Front page.

Cabot, Susan & Michael D. Rouse. *Images of America: Boone County.* Charleston SC: Arcadia Publishing, 1998.

Caldwell, Merrill S. "A Brief History of Slavery in Boone County, Kentucky." Boone County Historical Society. 21 June 1957.

Campbell, William Bruce, Sr. "Bullittsburg's Ministry of Faith 175 Years".

Capek, Michael. *Lively Stones: A Narrative History of The Belleview Baptist Church 1803-2003.* Tenn.: Tennessee Valley Publishing, 2002.

Carrollton Democrat newspaper. Published Carrollton, Ky.

Carskadden, Jeff & James Morton, *Where the Frolics and War Dances Are Held :The Indian Wars and The Early European Exploration and Settlement of Muskingum County and The Central Muskingum Valley.* Baltimore: Gateway Press, 1997.

Cason Family. *Timeless Recipes.* Tennessee: Fundcraft Publishing, 1993.

Cason, Josephine. "The Life of Thomas Zane Roberts". Greisser Collection. Burlington, Ky

Cason, Ralph Zane. *Daybook of Visitors.* Greisser Collection. Burlington, Ky.

Cason, Ralph Zane. Personal interviews. 1975

Chatfield, William H. *The Camargo Hunt Club.* Ohio: The C.J. Krekbriel Company, 2001.

Clare, Donald E. Jr. "Pikes Peak in Boone County." *Cincinnati.com/The Community Recorder.* 20 November 2006.

Clark, Thomas D. *The History of Kentucky.* New York: Prentice Hall, Inc., 1937.

Cleaves, Freeman. *Old Tippecanoe: William Henry Harrison and His Time.* Newtown, CT: American Political Biography Press, 1939.

Clore, Viola M. (Horton). *The Clore Family History.* (Copy at Boone County Library).

Conrad, William. "A Journal Into The Past". Boone County Board Of Education Community Education Program, 1984.

Conrad, William (Editor). Boone County: *The Top of Kentucky 1792-1992.* Ky.: Picture This! Books, 1992.

Conrad, William. "The History of Boone County Schools". Boone County Community Education Project. 30 June 1982.

Conrad, William. "The Vanishing Florence, Ky.", 2 June 1977.

Daily Recorder. Burlington, KY. 7-9 September 1889.

Deskins, Kathy. "Grandfather of Them All" *NK Communiqué.* Summer 1975.

Deskins, Kathy. "Uncle Tom's Cabin". *NK Innerviews.* August/September 1975.

Dickens, William Earl Jr. United On Mission : A History of The Northern Kentucky Baptist Association, 1803-1995.

Dinsmore Homestead Foundation. "The Basic History of The Dinsmore Foundation", August 1990.

Dinsmore, Julia Stockton. *Verses and Sonnets.* Kentucky: Picture This! Books, 1991.

Drury, John. "The National Road", *Midwest Heritage.* 1948.

Duvall, James R. "Bullittsburg Baptist Church Records 1795-1812".

Everhart, J.F. *The History of Muskingum County, Ohio.* Columbus, Ohio: J.F. Everhart & Co. 1882.

Fitzgerald, William. "Historian Speaks on Footprints in Kentucky Land". *Boone County Recorder.* 30 January 1964.

Fitzgerald, William. "The Origin of Boone County". *Boone County Recorder.* 2 January 1964.

Frost, Cathi Clore. The German Record ; *The First Four Generations of The Michael Clore Family.* Fredericksburg, Va.: Sheridan Books, 2005.

Greisser, Dorotha. *My Thoughts In Verse.* Volume I March 1933-April 1973. Privately published.

Greisser, Dorotha. Personal interviews. 2005-2006.

Greisser, Dorotha. "The Story of The Clock". Presentation at Florence Optimist and later at Heritage Bank. Original speech in author's possession.

Greisser, Dorotha and Gary Greisser, "Cason Clock Lives On At Heritage Bank." *The Boone County Recorder.* May 10, 1995, Vol. 120 No. 40 Page 3.

Grey, Zane. *Betty Zane.* NY: Grosset & Dunlap 1903.

Grey, Zane. *The Last Trail.* NY: Grosset & Dunlap. 1909.

Grey, Zane. *The Spirit of The Border.* Rosalyn, N.Y.: Grosset and Dunlop, 1971.

Gruber, Frank. *Zane Grey: A Biography.* Cleveland, Ohio: The World Publishing Company, 1970.

Hamilton, Deborah R. "Hemisphere Clock". *The Dixie News.* June 12, 1975.

Heiser, Alta Harvey. *West To Ohio.* Yellow Springs, Ohio: The Antioch Press, 1954.

Henry, Reginald Buchanan M.D., *Genealogies of the Families of the Presidents.* Rutland, Vermont: The Tuttle Company, 1935.

Hintzen, William & Joseph Roxby. *The Tales of Wheelings Frontier Era Heroic Age.* Apollo, Pa.: Clossom Press, 2000.

Huckabee, J.M. "A Horologist and Notes: Uncle Tom's Cabin... A Glimpse at His Diary". *American Horologist and Jeweler,* June 1969.

Jillson, Willard Rouse. *Big Bone Lick.* Louisville: The Standard Printing Co. Inc., 1936.

Johnson, Cave. "The Autobiography of Cave Johnson," 1845. Reprinted in *The Boone County Recorder,* Vol. 2 No. 19 Page 1, Feb 1, 1877, and Vol. 2 No. 20 Page 1, Feb. 8, 1877.

Kelly Elementary PTA (compiler). *Ancestry: Our Ohio River Heritage.* Indiana: Windmill Publications, Inc., 1996.

Kelly, Ruth. Personal interview. July 9, 1976.

Kennedy, General Robert P. "Isaac Zane: The White Eagle of The Wyandots". *The Ohio Magazine,* January 1, 1907, Vol. 2 No. 1.

Kentucky Heritage Commission. *Survey of Historic Sites In Kentucky: Boone County.* Newport, Ky.: Otto Printing Company, 1979.

Kirtley, Elizabeth McMullen. "Our Heritage: Burlington Baptist Church 150th Anniversary 1842-1992."

Kirtley, Elizabeth McMullen & Carlene Stephens. "History of East Bend Baptist Church 1819-1994."

Lee, Francis Bazley. *Genealogical and Memorial History of The State of New Jersey.* Lewis Historical Publishing Company, 1910.

Lloyd, Emma Rouse. *Clasping Hands With Generations Past.* Cincinnati: Wiesen-Hart Press, 1932.

Lutes, Ann. "A Brief History of Boone County, Kentucky". Boone County Historical Society, 1968.

Marion Record Volume XXXII No. 3, November 15, 1901, Page 1 Col. 2.

Marion Record Volume XXXIV No. 32, June 2, 1904, Page 1 Col. 5.

McClung, John A., *Sketches of Western Adventure*. (Philadelphia: Grigg and Elliott 1832, reprinted N.Y.: Arno Press and The New York Times, 1969).

McGehey, Howard, "Clock Built by Late Boone County Inventor Shows Movement," *The Kentucky Post,* December 10, 1931.

Meier, Emily. "Burlington Revealed: Historical Structures". History Senior Seminar. Thomas More College, 2003.

Middle Creek Church Records. Belleview Baptist Church, Belleview, Ky.

Neville, E.C. "Some Facts About Uncle Tom's Cabin". *The Hart County Herald.* August 28, 1969, page 12.

Norris, Dallas Howard. "The Reorganization of The Boone County School System". Thesis. University of Cincinnati, 1942.

Ramey, Jack. "It's Lonely Here". *The Cincinnati Enquirer.* May 8, 1954.

Ramey, Jack. "Rare Clock". *The Cincinnati Enquirer.* May 9, 1954. Section 3 Editorial Page 1 Col. 1.

Reis, Jim. "Beach A Popular Draw". *The Post.* July 18, 2005. 4K.

Reis, Jim. "Pieces of The Past". *The Kentucky Post.* 1988.

Reis, Jim. "Treks Won Fame for Zebulon Pike". *The Kentucky Post.* March 16, 1987.

Roberts, Martha Zane. Gravestone of Martha Zane Roberts, IOOF Cemetery, Carrollton, Kentucky.

Roberts, Roxanna Odell. *Family Bible.*

Roberts, Thomas Zane. *Diary.* Greisser Collection. Burlington. Ky.

Roberts, Thomas Zane. *Justice of The Peace Book.* Greisser Collection. Burlington. Ky.

Rouse, Jack. *The Civil War in Boone County, Kentucky.* Indiana: Windmill Publications, 1996.

Rowland, Isabella. Personal interviews. 2 February 2005; 20 June 2006; 21 June 2006.

Ryle High School PTSA. *A Peak Into The Past: A History of The Union and Richwood Areas.* Indiana: Windmill Publication, 1997.

Salt, John U. "Hand Made Wonder Clock of Boone County Hills". *The Daily Times Star.* Kentucky Edition, October 19, 1928, page 8 col. 3, 4.

Schaeffer, James F. *Piatt's Landing East Bend.* Cincinnati: The Cincinnati Gas and Electric Company, 1978.

Smith, Linda Mardis. *Historical Sketches of Northern Kentucky.* Erlanger, Ky: On Location Press, 1998.

Tanner, Paul. "A Brief History of Boone Circuit Court, Burlington, Ky. 1805-1933", 1989.

Tanner, Paul. "Acts Kentucky General Assembly Affecting Boone County Residents 1798-1890". 1996.

Tanner, Paul. "Slavery in Boone County, Kentucky and Its Aftermath", Frankfort, Ky., October 1986.

Theoret, Nanci. "Timepiece Burlington Man's Claim to Fame". *The Dixie News.* April 4, 1991, p. 13.

Thomas, Bill. "His Solar Clock's A Puzzler". *The Cincinnati Enquirer.* January 30, 1964.

Tucker, Whitney R., *The Descendants of The Presidents* (Charlotte, NC: Delmor Printing Company, 1975).

United States Corps of Engineers Louisville, Ky. District, *Flood Plain Information Ohio River Boone County, Kentucky,* 1967.

Utz, Reverend T.L. "History of Middle Creek Baptist Church 1874-1903".

Warner, Jennifer S. *Boone County, From Mastodons to The Millennium.* Boone County Bicentennial Committee. Ky., 1998.

Williams, Caroline. "A Spot Near Cincinnati". *The Enquirer.* January 25, 1948, p. 6.

Worrel, Stephen W. & Anne W. Fitzgerald. *Boone County, Kentucky County Court Orders 1799-1815.* Falls Church, Va., 1994.

Yealey, A.M. *History of Boone County, Kentucky.* Covington, Ky.: Holmes High School Press, 1960.

Zorn, Walter Lewis. *The Descendants of The Presidents of The United States.* Monroe, Michigan: Published by the author, 1955.

Time Keeper: Thomas Zane Roberts, a Kentucky Renaissance Man has the appearance of a recounting of the construction of the unique celestial clock that has long been considered the crowning achievement of its maker. However, Frohlich draws on over 30 years of research into the clock and the fascinating life of the man who built it. The author goes far beyond the often told "story of the clock" to explore the relationship of individual, family and community. He touches on the histories of communities ranging from Northern Kentucky to Zanesville, Ohio. T.Z. Roberts is revealed as a man of uncommon aptitude, vigor and love–for God, life and earth. Frohlich's consideration of Roberts' love interests and coded diary entries is particularly fascinating. Roberts' appended poems and short stories are available here for the first time in over 130 years. With a complete picture of the man, the reader sees the "celestial clock of Middle Creek" more than a book about a man and his clock, it is a work of interest to genealogists, local historians and horologists alike.

Matthew E. Becher, Staff
Boone County Historic Preservation Review Board

This book provides deep insight into the life, accomplishments, and family of Thomas Zane Roberts, a complex and creative man who spent his entire life in the Middle Creek area of Northern Kentucky. The author provides answers to intriguing questions, based on years of research.

Marty McDonald, Ph.D.
Executive Director, Dinsmore Homestead Foundation

The author, Tony Frohlich, has captured the story of an exceptional man, T.Z. Roberts, and a special community, the Middle Creek area, in this comprehensive writing. For the first time T.Z. Roberts has been acknowledged as a multi-talented individual who characterized the industry and strength of Boone County during its growth in the 20th century.

Judge Bruce Ferguson